Digital Visual Art Education

Robert W. Sweeny

Digital Visual Art Education

Making, Learning, and Teaching with Digital Media

PETER LANG
New York - Berlin - Bruxelles - Chennai - Lausanne - Oxford

Library of Congress Cataloging-in-Publication Data

Names: Sweeny, Robert W., author.
Title: Digital visual art education: making, learning, and teaching with digital media / Robert W. Sweeny.
Description: New York: Peter Lang, [2024] | Includes bibliographical references and index.
Identifiers: LCCN 2024000916 (print) | LCCN 2024000917 (ebook) | ISBN 9781433195648 (hardback) | ISBN 9781433195624 (ebook) | ISBN 9781433195631 (epub)
Subjects: LCSH: New media art–Philosophy. | New media art–Study and teaching. | Art and society.
Classification: LCC NX456.5.N49 S94 2024 (print) | LCC NX456.5.N49 (ebook) | DDC 776.071–dc23/eng/20240201
LC record available at https://lccn.loc.gov/2024000916
LC ebook record available at https://lccn.loc.gov/2024000917
DOI 10.3726/b21753

Bibliographic information published by the Deutsche Nationalbibliothek.
The German National Library lists this publication in the German National Bibliography; detailed bibliographic data is available on the Internet at http://dnb.d-nb.de.

Cover design by Peter Lang Group AG

ISBN 9781433195648 (hardback)
ISBN 9781433195624 (ebook)
ISBN 9781433195631 (epub)
DOI 10.3726/b21753

Published by Peter Lang Publishing Inc., New York, USA
info@peterlang.com— www.peterlang.com

This publication has been peer reviewed.

To Marj: For the generative node
And may the FLorida BOMbeRS roll on and on…

CONTENTS

LIST OF FIGURES

PREFACE

This was written when the COVID-19 global pandemic was raging across the globe, and my current home state of Pennsylvania. The weather this summer was hot and was made hotter due to the requirement that all Pennsylvanians wear a mask in public. For the first time in fifteen years, I will not return to the classroom in the Fall, as I have been awarded a sabbatical to work on this book project. The Fall semester will bring ten-thousand-plus students to this small town in a few weeks. With this influx will come uncertainty and fear, and perhaps the hope that things will return to normal—a normal that did not include face shields, social distancing, and virtual instruction.

This was written while protests for racial justice spread across the US. The killing of George Floyd on May 25, 2020, at the hands of police in Minneapolis MN, sparked protests that have expressed rage at this specific injustice, as well as serving as a platform for larger calls for the defunding of the police and legal justice reform. These protests have aligned with the COVID-19 pandemic in a number of ways. Both point out that systemic racism has resulted in Black and brown people in the US being more likely to die from COVID-19, and more likely to die at the hands of the police.

These simultaneous intersecting events have forced many art educators to rethink their traditional practices. They are restructuring methods of interaction and engagement to incorporate social distancing and virtual instruction. They are critically examining the relationship between their practices and issues of social justice and racial inequality. Many are undoubtedly concerned with the history oppression of Black and brown people in the United States that continues in the present, and how this influences art educational practices. While these issues are opening space for long-neglected conversations to be had, and now that distance education is more common than ever, it is time for art, design, and media educators to embrace art that speaks to racial injustice and oppression, and that is also made to be viewed at a distance. Art that is "born digital."[1]

Digital art has always been multifaceted. The term fails to grasp the multitudinous styles and approaches represented by artists working with digital technologies. There have been various terms used to describe these approaches: computer art, interactive art, multimedia art, hypertextual art, new media art, net.art, and post-internet art, to name but a few. Net.art might be the best example of art that is made to be viewed at a distance as it simultaneously speaks to social issues. The beginnings of net.art can be traced back to the early 1990's, when the World Wide Web was starting to open up to a wider audience. The term itself is credited to Slovenian artist Vuk Cosic, who reported that it was the result of a computer glitch.[2] Early examples of net.art were primarily text-based, due to the data limitations of the early World Wide Web. As home computers became more powerful, net.art began to incorporate images, eventually incorporating sound and video. With the rise of mobile computing came the ability for place-based visualizations, usually in the form of augmented reality such as Pokemon Go.

Net.art tends to be made by artists who identify as white. This is not remarkable, considering that an estimated 85% of artists represented in US museums in the early 21st century are white.[3] However, it does challenge the idea that the internet was initially promised to be a space for increased diversity, representation, and visibility. While this disparity exists, there have been a number of important net.art works made by people of color. Artists, educators, and researchers who are looking for way to open up important conversations about race at the same time that they are challenged by the lack of face-to-face contact can find excellent opportunities for engagement through net.art and artists.[4]

Digital artistic practices can provide opportunities for artists, educators, and researchers to better understand issues such as these. I have started with these examples because they are relevant to our current age. It is my explicit goal, throughout this text, to make reference to digital visual artists of color, as they are all too often left out of conversations of new media theory and practice. I do this as an art educator who identifies as white, heterosexual, and cis-male, who is well-aware of the privileges that this identification has provided. This emphasis will not change systemic racism or patriarchal structures that have been in place for centuries. I am not sure exactly what this emphasis will change, but I know that I must use the platform that I have to acknowledge these individuals and hope that discussions of digital art are more equitable in the future.

Most importantly, digital visual artists of color tend to make the type of art that I have found compelling for the past fifteen years: art that is confrontational, art that is confusing, art that uses a variety of technologies to point out the dysfunctional aspects of systems that are designed to function at the most efficient level possible. This self-reflexivity is one of the most intriguing attributes of digital visual art (Manovich, 2000; Crowther, 2008). Digital visual art is the term that I will use throughout this book to describe art that is made with, or about, digital media. I am using this term as it is arguably less burdened that some of the other, more specific terms that have been used in the recent past: interactive media, computer art, new media, net.art. I am using the word visual in the phrase, so that it references more traditional works of art, as well as digital visual culture, even though many works of digital visual art downplay or eliminate the visual aspects of the work being presented.

Digital visual culture is, simply put, the myriad cultural forms of visual expression that make use of digital technologies. Digital visual culture encompasses many interrelated fields and practices; at its core, digital visual culture is an offshoot of visual culture. My own research has dealt with intersections between visual culture topics as diverse as surveillance, performance art and reality TV, data visualization, and videogames. I have written about each of these topics as they relate to art educational history, theories of curriculum design, and pre-K-12 pedagogical approaches. As I have written about each of these topics, I have been forced to look outside of the literature that exists within the field of art education. Through this process I have concluded that digital visual art cannot be adequately understood by only looking to art educational research.

This is the overarching argument that informs the development of Digital Visual Art Education as presented herein. This interdisciplinary research approach has led to this book, which takes up and makes use of theories from the fields of media studies, digital communications, philosophy, cultural studies, as well as art and design education. The latter tend to frame aspects of the digital as they relate to pedagogical implementation. Theories that concern the digital in art education often derive from this last field, although you can find those that are influenced by the previously mentioned fields as well. There is a need for research that draws together these two types of resources: the applied and the theoretical. This is the balance that art educators often find themselves striving to maintain. This book attempts to strike this balance in a manner that does not either simplify or obfuscate. As I have been able to reflect upon my previous research writings in the field of art education, I have seen where they have successfully drawn together theory and practice, which has always been my goal. I also now see where my writings have missed the mark, either by weighing too heavily on one approach or the other. I am writing primarily for educators and researchers working in higher education. It is most relevant for those who are doing research on digital media as it relates to art educational practices and processes, but in addition it is also relevant for pre-K-12 practitioners, community art organizers, museum educators, and digital media students.

I am interested in analyzing specific qualities of digital visual culture in this book, and how these qualities can be placed into a theoretical framework useful for research that takes myriad forms and is located in numerous sites. The qualities that I identified previously– temporality, the theory and practice dyad, and multilinearity—are not unique to digital visual culture. However, they are more common to this field of study than to visual culture in general, primarily due to the nature of digital media. I am not interested in arresting the dynamic aspects of digital media, isolating them and immobilizing them in order to study them. I am more interested in surveying them as they currently operate, looking to the influences that have brought them to where they now are, and speculating as to where they might lead. These motivations, when taken as a whole, speak less to the general contours of a digital visual culture, and more to the study of digital visual culture within the spaces of art education. As such, I am calling this book, and the approaches contained within, Digital Visual Art Education.

This book presents detailed interdisciplinary analyses of digital media as they are currently being created and presented by visual artists. It places these works into a theoretical framework that is useful for research in fields such as art education, media studies, studio art, and design education. The primary goal of the book is to emphasize the multidisciplinary aspects of digital visual art, and to propose a field of study that is unique to this type of art. Digital

Visual Art Education combines theories from media studies, such as temporality and multilinearity, and beings them into a dialogue with sociological theories such as feminist New Materialism and Critical Race Theory. In doing so, the complex social and cultural aspects of digital visual art can be better understood. The book presents a select analysis of digital visual art as it is currently being produced and disseminated, looking to the numerous influences that have brought it into being, and speculates as to where it might lead for future researchers, artists, and designers.

The analysis presented in each of the chapters of this book is unique; each chapter will build upon similar themes while allowing for the identification of the specific qualities of the digital visual artists and artworks described within. These chapters build upon the research and teaching that I have been engaged with over the past 25 years, as a PK-12 art educator and university professor. Each study is presented as a separate chapter, which can be taken by itself as research on a specific technology or approach. The chapters can also be read in series; I will identify overarching themes and concepts in each chapter that, together, speak to the larger concept of a Digital Visual Art Education. The book begins with an analysis of the concept of digital visuality. The chapters that follow are organized around the four themes that emerge from digital visuality: Interconnectedness, Indeterminacy, Interactivity, and Intersectionality. Each chapter features research drawn primarily from Art Education, Design Education, and Media Studies. Additionally, I have included citations from fields such as Art History, Art Criticism, Continental Philosophy, Information Science, Cybernetics, and Sociology, in order to expand the discussion for a wider audience, providing additional context for these intersections that speak to research and creative approaches that I am calling Digital Visual Art Education.

Notes

1 Patton, R. & Knochel, A. (2017). VAR Born Digital Editorial. *Visual Arts Research*, 43(1), –Xiv. doi:10.5406/visuartsrese.43.1.000v
2 http://www.easylife.org/netart/
3 https://news.artnet.com/market/new-study-shows-us-art-museums-grappling-with-diversity-1467256
4 Much of this art has been archived at Rhizome.org. Rhizome has published a guide for activists using digital media as a space of resistance, which is available at https://rhizome.org/editorial/2020/jun/03/digital-resources-for-a-movement-against-police-violence/

· 1 ·

DIGITAL VISUALITY

The eyes have been used to signify a perverse capacity—honed to perfection in the history of science tied to militarism, capitalism, colonialism, and male supremacy—to distance the knowing subject from everybody and everything in the interests of unfettered power…The "eyes" made available in modern technological sciences shatter any idea of passive vision; these prosthetic devices show us that all eyes, including our own organic ones, are active perceptual systems, building in translations and specific ways of seeing, that is, ways of life. (Haraway, 2001)

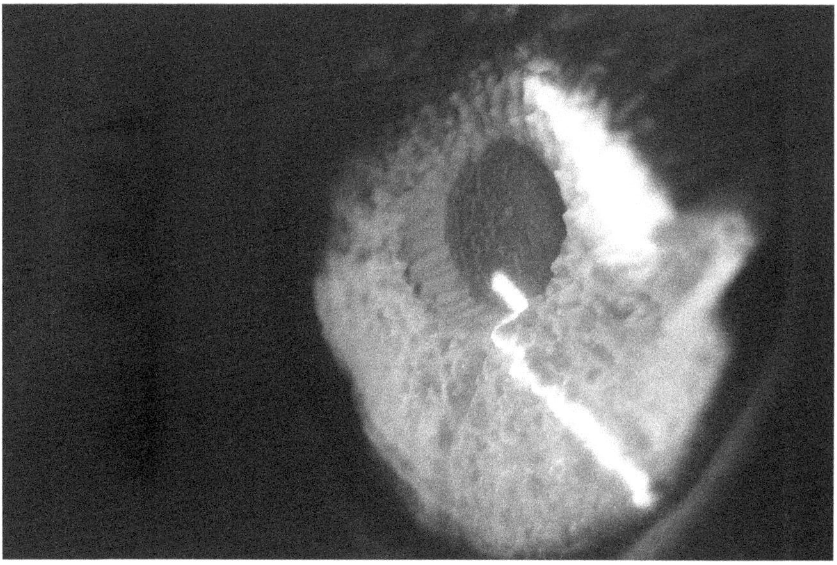

Figure 1.1. Eyes (2018), by Yoon Chung Han

Source: http://yoonchunghan.com/portfolio/Eyes.html [accessed 8/16/2023]. Used with permission of the artist.

Digital Visual Art Education is being proposed as a set of research themes and approaches that look to the implications for digital visual art within many disciplines and on a broad social and cultural scale. The primary goal is to identify research practices and themes that can assist art, design, and media educators as they conduct creative and critical research with digital media. This book begins with an outlining of the concept of digital visuality and the related topics of interconnectedness, indeterminacy, interactivity, and intersectionality. This theory of digital visuality will take into account the unique, dynamic, and challenging aspects of digital visual art, using the topics previously mentioned to address a number of social and cultural issues; specifically identity, materiality, and power. Specific works of digital visual art from a variety of media will be analyzed so that the complexities of digital visual art can be better understood. In the concluding chapter, the ways that art educators, artists, designers, researchers, and theorists can make use of these analytical forms will be discussed.

Throughout this text, I will rely upon the following terms: *Digital media* will refer to the techniques and tools that are used to make *digital visual art*. As I mentioned in the forward, there are many varieties of digital visual art: computer art, interactive art, multimedia art, hypertext, new media art, net.art, and post-internet art are only some of the terms that have been used since the early use of computer systems in the mid 20th century. There are concerns with each of the words that make up the term digital visual art. The term "digital" means next to nothing in an era where everything from refrigerators to family pets are interconnected by and through technological networks. Visual is problematic when there are plenty of examples of art specifically from the 20th and 21st century that are "post-retinal," to borrow a term from Marcel Duchamp. And the word art is perhaps the most challenging to use here, as it is clearly open to relentless subjective interpretation and cultural definition.

As indicated by the opening quote from Donna Haraway, in this chapter I will scrutinize the relationship between digital technologies and vision, including those that might seem untouched by the effects of networked digital technologies. I will connect the concepts of interconnectedness, indeterminacy, interactivity, and intersectionality to this theory of digital visuality, to describe how it operates within a digital visual work of art. As I stated in the introduction, my goal is to propose a Digital Visual Art Education that is drawn from digital works of art. Whenever possible, I will focus on works made by artists of color, as they have been left out of so many important conversations in digital media theory. This approach will be mirrored in each of the chapters to follow. *Eyes* (2018) by Yoon Chung Han is a work that speaks to the complexities of vision in a digitally mediated world.

Yoon Chung Han is a digital visual artist whose work spans multiple disciplines and utilizes numerous approaches. From her website: "Yoon C Han is an interaction designer, multimedia artist, and researcher. Her research includes data visualization, biometric data visualization and sonification, new interface for musical expression, and mobile user experience design" (n.p.). Her 2018 work titled Eyes speaks to many of these issues: ""Eyes" is an interactive biometric data art that transforms human's iris data into musical sound and 3D animated image" (n.p.). In this work, the viewer scans their eye using a specially made scanner. These scans are processed by the computer and are displayed as both 3D visualization and sound piece. Selected visualizations are then 3D printed and displayed in the gallery space, with the related audio information playing in the space. For Yoon, the work functions as both art and data visualization:

> It has potentials to lead the new way of interpreting complicated dataset with the audiovisual output. More importantly, aesthetically beautiful, mesmerizing and a bit uncanny valley-effected artwork can create personalized art experience and multi-modal interaction. Multi-sensory interpretations of the iris data art can lead a new opportunity to reveal users' narratives and create their own "sonic signature", which will be able to trigger a new way of interaction in the fields of art and science (n.p.).

The multifaceted aspects of this work speak to digital visuality. This work uses a number of media forms that I will be analyzing at various points throughout the book: data visualization, 3D printing, sound art. The ability for the computer to translate data into numerous different forms is a hallmark of new media art (Manovich, 2001). This quality is undoubtedly familiar to anyone who has access to contemporary digital technologies. Even the most rudimentary smartphone can send and receive text, image, and sound data. It can translate the spoken word to text and can embed visual images with data regarding location and time. The impact of digital technologies has been an area of research from the initial development of the Cathode Ray Tube (CRT). Researchers have looked at the ways that digital images change peripheral vision (Varma, 1992) and how gamma rays from digital displays impact sleep patterns and attentiveness (DePriest, 2018).

It is clear that the projection of digital information is different from other types of visual information, such as the printed page, or human sight in general. What I am interested in discussing with regards to visuality and digital visual art is how these works might engage the viewer in novel forms of looking and seeing. Additionally, I am interested in how digital visual works of art might represent biological and sociocultural aspects of vision. These are interrelated concepts that will form the basis of digital visuality as it is being used in this book.

Visual Culture scholar Nicholas Mirzoeff (2011) speaks to the history of visuality as such: "Visuality is an old word for an old project. It is not a trendy theory-word meaning the totality of all visual images and devices, but it is in fact an early nineteenth-century term, meaning the visualization of history" (p. 474). In this definition, we see a specific reading of visuality that speaks to the power of visualization, and the ability to control through these mechanisms. As I will show, this understanding of visuality is crucial for the theorization of Digital Visual Art Education that I am proposing in this book. The digital visuality that I will be discussing should be thought of in two ways. The first form should be thought of as being primarily theoretical, and is related to the content of the work, the intent of the artist, and the interpretation of the viewer. Here, digital visuality occurs within the networks of production and distribution. This is a visuality that is structural. The second form of visuality should be thought of as being primarily formal; it is related to the form of the work, and the mode of presentation. To consider the digital visuality of an object, action, or concept, the visibility of the experience must be taken into account.

As Art Historian Norman Bryson (1988) writes:

> Between the subject and the world is inserted the entire sum of discourses which make up visuality, the cultural construct; and makes visuality different from vision, the notion of unmediated visual experience. Between retina and world is inserted a screen of signs, a screen consisting of all the multiple discourses on vision built into the social arena.

The aspects of visuality identified by Bryson here are drawn into question by Haraway, as the introductory quote indicates. "The notion of an unmediated experience" that biological vision represents is simply that. A notion. Even the simple act of wearing eyeglasses is a prosthetic augmentation of "natural" vision. And while eyeglasses might not be considered a cultural construct, they are certainly an advanced technology. This technology is one that has been normalized to the point where eyeglass wearers might consider them to be part of their bodies. They exist as equal parts appendage, fashion statement, and tool.

Yoon describes the programs that are used in *Eyes* (2018) as "tools" in the project description. The specific tools that she uses in this piece are D3.js, Three.js, and Max/MSP.[1] The citation of programs that are used in works of digital visual art and data visualization is a common practice in these fields like the reference to the materials used in gallery and museum-based works of visual art. However, if one considers works of art in the Western tradition, as well as works of design and craft, the tools would rarely, if ever, be shown as part of the finished work. The tools are what are used to produce the work, and as such they remain in the background. The tools are not visible. However, the tools contribute greatly to the visuality of the work.

Digital visual works of art are generally no different. As Christiane Paul writes in her curatorial statement for Programmed: Rules, Codes, and Choreographies in Art, 1965—2018 (Whitney Museum of American Art):

> Walk into any given gallery or museum today, and one will presumably encounter work that used digital technologies as a tool at some point in its production, whether videos that were filmed and edited using digital cameras and post-production software, sculptures designed using computer-aided design, or photographs as digital prints, to name just a few examples. Yet these works are not typically understood as digital art per se, since they use digital technologies as a production tool rather than a medium. Instead, digital art might be defined as art that explores digital technologies as a medium by making use of its medium's key features, such as its real-time, interactive, participatory, generative, and variable characteristics, or by reflecting upon the nature and impact of digital technologies (n.p.).

The tools that Paul lists here can often be reapplied to digital visual works of art, in a reflexive manner. This can be seen as an extension of the Modernist attempt to demystify the artistic process and democratize the product. In Introduction to net.art (1994–1999) (1999), Natalie Bookchin and Alexei Shulgin describe net.art[2] as "The Ultimate Modernism" (n.p.). In their outline format, the third point is titled "Realization over Theorization," and it reads as follows:

> a. The utopian aim of closing the ever widening gap between art and everyday life, perhaps, for the first time, was achieved and became a real, everyday and even routine practice.
> b. Beyond institutional critique: whereby an artist/individual could be equal to and on the same level as any institution or corporation.
> c. The practical death of the author

As Bookchin and Shulgin suggest, net.art is an extension of the utopian impulse that motivated many Modernist artists in the late 19th and early 20th centuries. In this utopian impulse can be found the attempt to demystify the process of making art and democratize the distribution of the product. Allowing the audience to have access to the tools used to make the work is a gesture that points to both of these goals. The effects of this process, as Bookchin and Shulgin (1999) argue, are inherently critical: When art and everyday life are one and the same, then the individual and the institution could be made equal, as could the artist and the viewer. The visibility of the process behind the product, therefore, has a sociopolitical component that must be acknowledged when discussing digital visuality. Digital visuality would acknowledge a subjective point of view that does not privilege the artist, but it also does not flatten the experience into a distributed network where all interpretations are valid and all meanings are equal. The point of view of the artist would be a hub, through which the viewer can perceive the work in a particular manner. Another hub might be the institution that supports the work, and a third hub might be found in the groups or organizations that provide technical support for the work. This is the model of the interconnected, decentralized network that I described in the forward, and it is the model that relates to visual experiences in a Digital Visual Art Education. The relationship between visuality and visibility in digital visual works of art leads to the first aspect of digital visuality to be discussed: interconnectedness.

Interconnectedness

Contemporary digital media differ from previous media forms in and through their interconnectedness. The proliferation of digital networks that have developed alongside the internet speaks to a quality that distinguishes interconnected digital media from those which are not connected in such a manner. In the early 21st century, digital media are linked in ways that might have been previously unthinkable (Castells, 1996: Johnson, 2001). These linkages represent a profound shift in the ways that digital media are used, shared, and applied to the creation of digital works of art.

As I have previously argued (Sweeny, 2015), the model of the decentralized network seems to best describe the ways in which contemporary digital media connect with one another. Decentralized networks are composed of individual nodes, which connect with one another through hubs that channel information throughout the system. They provide the greatest amount of flexibility and stability, when compared with either centralized networks, where all flows are channeled through one singular hub, or distributed networks, where all nodes are connected to each other.[3]

The concept of the decentralized network owes much to the research conducted by Paul Baran (1964) at RAND Corporation in the early 1960's. In his research, Baran was looking for ways to route electronic military communications around damaged networks, such as in the case of a catastrophic event such as a nuclear attack. He found that a robust distributed network was able to maintain communicational integrity much better than either centralized networks, where all communication flows through a single point, or decentralized networks, where communication is channeled through hubs that direct information flow between all points. His research led to the development of cellular communication, distributed computing, and was central to the fields of Cybernetics, Complexity Theory, and Information Science.

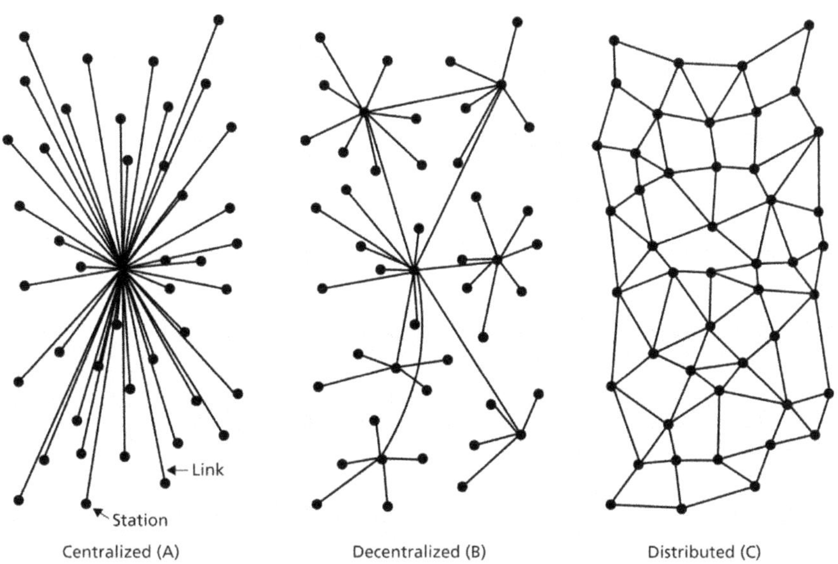

Figure 1.2. Network Diagram (1964), Paul Baran/RAND Corporation

Source: Baran, P. (1964) On Distributed Communications Networks. IEEE Transactions of the Professional Technical Group on Communication Systems. Volume CS-12, Number 1. RAND Corporation. Used with permission of the publisher.

Although Baran placed the greatest value for electronic communication in the distributed network, I have previously argued that the decentralized network can offer artists, educators, and theorists a robust model for thinking about the relationship between digital media and art education. Decentralized interconnectedness is the primary concept that I will use to analyze digital art throughout this book. Previously, I have discussed the importance of decentralization in the fields of philosophy, technology, and education as they relate to new media works of art in particular. And, while centralized, decentralized, and distributed network models can help in the understanding of a wide variety of complex sociocultural fields and formations, the decentralized network is specifically well-suited to discussing contemporary digital media, as they are linked in and through these types of connections. Decentralization can help art, design, and media educators to better understand, and therefore teach from, digital visual works of art. The shift here is important: in my previous work I had focused on new media art as a general category. Here I am using the term digital visual art in order to be more inclusive, as mentioned earlier. I am also attempting to avoid some of the discussions regarding historical framing and nomenclature. Important though these discussions may be in the discussion of digital visual art, they are of secondary importance in this text.

The way that I am using interconnectedness in this theory of digital visuality relies upon the model of the decentralized network, and specifically the ability for information that flows through this network to provide the user with feedback. In the initial routing network that Baran (1964) called a hot potato network, message blocks were sent through the electronic network, which was composed of circuits that transmitted electronic signals through switching hubs that could direct the flow of electricity. When a message block, or packet, passes through a node, this passage is recorded by both the node and the packet. Nodes documented each of the previous nodes that the packed had visited. Eventually, the nodes of the network would have a record of the dimensions of the network structure as a whole and would be able to guide packets based on the optimal path available. Each packet, as it passes through the individual nodes of the network, is coded with information by the node that is passes through. Each node, in turn, tracks the previous nodes that the packet has visited, compiling a list that determines the most efficient routes.

This is the process of feedback that gave the decentralized communications networks the ability to route around damaged nodes. Baran's work was prompted by the possibility of a nuclear attack in the early 1960's, but it was influenced by his research into reducing noise in missile guidance communicational systems (Wieczorek, 2020). The feedback loops that could route around noise in the system, or complete blockages, were only made possible through redundant pathways in the network; the distributed network is the most redundant, as all nodes are connected to each other. This structure is the most stable, but the redundancies in the distributed network are only necessary in the case of a catastrophic attack on the system, such as in the case of a nuclear attack. In applications that take place outside of the imminent threat of nuclear warfare, a decentralized network would combine the best of the stable, centralized network and the flexible distributed network, relying upon feedback loops for communication to take place.

Eyes (2018) uses the image of the human eye to make a statement about vision and digital technology, which is ascertained by the senses of the viewer: sight, sound, and perhaps touch. This is a type of feedback loop that is informed by the dynamic qualities of the decentralized network. In this reflexive process of feedback, which is now commonly discussed in fields such as Information Systems, we can begin to track the ways that vision itself is addressed. The reproduction of the eye as scan, sound, and sculpture in *Eyes* (2018) is accomplished by the computer program that is running in the background of the work, out of sight. As stated previously, the information provided by the artist lists the programs used while it also references assistance with 3D Visualization Implementation that was provided by Praful Surve. In the work of Keith and Mendhi Obadike, for example, digital processes are often made visible to the viewer of the work in a manner that allows for the scrutinization of the process to take place.

Keith and Mendhi Obadike are artists based in the US who started making internet-based art in the mid 1990's:

> One of their earliest pieces was My Hands Wishful Thinking (2000), a memorial for Amadou Diallo, an innocent man who was killed by the New York Police Department. From 2001–2003 they created a suite of "Black.Net.Art Actions". This suite included Blackness for Sale (2001), Keeping Up Appearances (2001), The Interaction of Coloreds (2002/2018), and The Pink of Stealth (2003). These early works led to their later explorations of code, "social filters", and databases (Obadike, n.p.).

This work seems particularly relevant twenty years later, considering how the Black Lives Matter movement and the COVID-19 global pandemic have brought the brutal effects of systemic racism to international attention starting in 2020. Art educators who are reexamining issues of racial justice in their practices, and who are forced to consider hybrid forms of instruction, including distance education, should consider works such as *My Hands Wishful Thinking*[4] (2001). This "internet memorial piece" presents the viewer with 41 affirmative statements addressed to Amadou Diallo, who was shot and killed by the New York City Police in 1999. The police fired 41 shots at Diallo, with 19 of them striking his body. As the Obadikes' write:

> in this piece there is one thought to counteract each bullet fired. the words are wishful thinking in the present tense. these thoughts reject the negative forces directed against us, the survivors, african people in the united states. making this work is an enactment of our will to survive (n.p.).

This piece, which is archived as a digital video, utilized a simple Flash video to show a hand with the complexion of someone of African descent raising up and down. Additional hands surrounding the central moving image display a wallet, alluding to the fact that police thought Diallo was holding a weapon, when he was in fact holding his wallet. The piece is impactful and stark, but the text statements speak to the promises of racial equality: "Rather than an expression of trauma, loss, and violence, this deeply moving work of net.art activism places hope in the power of collectivity and a future without racist violence" (Knustad, n.p.).

As I will suggest throughout this book, the concept of the decentralized network can allow us to draw out relevant aspects of digital visual art that are relevant to the theorizing of a Digital Visual Art Education. Digital visual artworks such as *My Hands Wishful Thinking* (2001) open up space for different forms of interaction, as Manovich (2001) outlines. New media art in this regard generally creates spaces for interactivity, in that the viewer can change visual and audio components of the piece in unique and idiosyncratic ways. When searching for this specific piece, a link to a different version of the piece came up in my search engine. This version shows the same image of a raising hand surrounded by repeated hands, some holding wallets. However, when you click on the central hand, a sound file downloads and plays. This sound file is a mashup of a number of audio clips that play overlapping samples, with various voices stating "41 shots fired," "19," and "No Justice, No Peace."

The fact that there at least two versions of this internet memorial piece demonstrates the indeterminacy of digital visual art. One can view the pieces side-by-side, combining the text from one and the sounds from the other to create an entirely new piece, which also relates to the ability for one to easily remix digital media (Miller, 2004). In fact, the Electronic Literature as a Model of Creativity and Innovation in Practice (ELMCIP) webpage on the piece includes the source code. This would allow the viewer to not only see the code that makes up the piece; it also would allow them to modify the code if they had the technical know-how and artistic inclination.

While it is easy to speak to the technical aspects of the piece, it is not as easy to confront the content of the work. The violence that the work speaks to is brutal, just as the sound piece is constructed in a jarring manner. The echoes of the cries of "No Justice, No Piece" still can be heard in the streets of the United States, some 20 years later. At the end of the sound piece, a voice says "I still want to know why this happened." We can ask this question about Breonna Taylor, Auhmad Arbury, George Floyd, or Tyre Nichols to name only a few recent Black victims of US police brutality. Because this piece has been archived, both by the artists and by groups such as the ELMCIP, viewers of the work can be reminded of what work still needs to be done with regards to social justice and racial equality. In the different versions of the work, there are both suffering and hope to be found. The sound piece is abrasive, while the text-based version represents a form of wishful thinking, as the title states. If one is interested in interpreting the meaning of the work, then they would undoubtedly need to consider both versions simultaneously. The meaning shifts based upon the version that is viewed, and in this indeterminacy we can see the dynamic qualities of the decentralized network.

Indeterminacy

> As digital technologies have infiltrated almost all aspects of art-making today, many artists, curators, and theorists have pronounced an age of "post-digital" and "post-internet" art. These terms attempt to describe a condition of artworks that are conceptually and practically shaped by the internet and digital processes—taking their language for granted—yet often manifest in the material form of objects such as paintings, sculptures, or photographs that speak about the digital medium and would not be possible without it (Paul, 2020)

The second concept that will inform the approach to Digital Visual Art Education outlined in this book is indeterminacy. To be indeterminate is to be vague; to not know the precise characteristics of a condition or a concept. It is related to the notion of incompleteness. However, they are not identical terms. Something can be complete, while the exact qualities are not quantifiable. The human body is made of a complete set of components; organs, bones, fluids and fibers that can be numbered and measured. However, the ways that these parts combine and interact are often beyond the ability to be fully apprehended.

The notion of the post-digital speaks to the indeterminacy that is often found in digital media art. The post-digital is, as with my previous concepts, not specific to digital visual art. However, the post-digital speaks directly to aspects of digital visual art that can help in the theorization of a Digital Visual Art Education. The concept of the post-digital was first conceived within the field of electronic music (Cascone, 2000), but was quickly adopted by theorists and visual artists. In general, post-digital art makes reference to pre-digital technologies while also operating within systems where digital technologies are ubiquitous (Cramer, 2014).

Post-digital art is instructive in this regard, as it does away with previous binary forms of categorization. While it is instructive, it is not general enough to warrant incorporation in the title of the approach to research being presented in this book. Post-digital visual art is a category that will be used throughout the book, alongside other types of visual art. The necessity of such a shift is persuasively argued by Cramer (2014):

> The everyday colloquial definition of "digital" embraces the fiction (or rather: the abstraction) of the disembodied nature of digital information processing. The colloquial use of "digital" also tends to be metonymical, so that anything connected literally or figuratively to computational electronic devices—even a camera tripod—can nowadays be called "digital". This notion, mainly cultivated by product marketing and advertising, has been unquestioningly adopted by the "digital humanities" (as illustrated by the very term "digital humanities"). On the other hand, "post-digital" art, design and media—whether or not they should technically be considered post-digital—challenge such uncritical notions of digitality, thus making up for what often amounts to a lack of scrutiny among "digital media" critics and scholars (p. 20).

As Elkins (2003) writes: "Visual studies is in just as much danger of becoming alienated from the details of computer hardware and software as art history is in danger of forgetting the meanings that emerge from making." The ability for art educators, media theorists and designers to take into account multiple indeterminate aspects of digital visual art, including those that might seem far from the digital, is precisely what a Digital Visual Art Education can provide. The primary theoretical reference point for understanding indeterminacy here can be located in A Thousand Plateaus (1987), written by Gilles Deleuze and Felix Guattari. In this text, Deleuze and Guattari describe a nomadic form of ontology that is less beholden to Western concepts of rationality and order. Instead, they look to a wide-ranging number of sources to construct their nomadic approach which is based in the notion of the rhizome.

In their descriptions of the rhizome Deleuze and Guattari make comparisons to hierarchical, root-like systems, using the examples of the map and the tracing. As they propose, the map is a rhizome, as it extends itself laterally, providing openings that lead to the development of new rhizomes. The tracing is always a representation of the network that is being analyzed; it is always an abstraction, while the map is an independent entity unto itself:

> The rhizome is altogether different, a map and not a tracing. Make a map, not a tracing. The orchid does not reproduce the tracing of the wasp; it forms a map with the wasp, in a rhizome. What distinguishes the map from the tracing is that it is entirely oriented toward an experimentation in contact with the real. The map does not reproduce an unconscious closed in upon itself; it constructs the unconscious. It fosters connections between fields, the removal of blockages on bodies without organs, the maximum opening of bodies without organs onto a plane of consistency. It is itself a part of the rhizome. The map is open and connectable in all of its dimensions; it is detachable, reversible, susceptible to constant modification. It can be torn, reversed, adapted to any kind of mounting, reworked by an individual, group, or social formation. It can be drawn on a wall, conceived of as a work of art, constructed as a political action or as a meditation (pp. 12–13).

As they continue their description of the map and the tracing, Deleuze and Guattari complicate this binary by suggesting that the map and the tracing are interconnected, just as the rhizome can form root-like structures, only to shift back to rhizomatic formations. The rhizome as theorized by Deleuze and Guattari stands as a compelling model for a nomadic form of writing, thinking, and being. In the field of new media art, the rhizome has been taken up by a number of artists, theorists, art historians, and art educators. It is, perhaps, represented most prominently through the new media art archive that takes the term as its name: Rhizome.org. Rhizome.org was founded in 1996 by artist and curator Mark Tribe. Initially serving as a platform for digital art and media, it gradually evolved into an online archive for new media art. It currently is affiliated with the New Museum of Contemporary Art, located in New York City. Rhizome.org in many ways represents the shifting nature of the rhizome as theorized by Deleuze and Guattari. It operates as a web-based outlet for new media art and theory, while it also maintains a physical presence, organizing lectures and exhibitions. In this manner, Rhizome.org is a decentralized network that is inherently indeterminate and variable.

Manovich (2001) argues that variability is central to new media works of art: "A new media object is not something fixed once and for all, but something that can exist in different, potentially infinite versions" (p. 36).[5] In terms of digital visual works of art, variability can be thought of as being presenting the viewer with numerous visual images simultaneously, which they can then customize in an interactive manner. The impact of such visual simultaneity can be pleasing, or overwhelming, or perhaps it might make no impact whatsoever, depending on the experiences that the viewer has had with such experiences. The sheer volume of photographs online, for example, has allowed photographers to work with previously inconceivable amounts of images, without ever touching a camera (Cole, 2015). The use of readymade images certainly changes the way that the relationship between the artist and the art produced is thought of, especially with regards to traditional notions of creativity and originality. While artists have always borrowed from various sources and time periods (Navas, 2018), digital technologies allow for this process to take place on an unprecedented scale.

While not universal, many digital visual artists included in the Rhizome database freely share the tools and the codes that they use to make their work, with the implicit understanding that viewers might reinterpret them in a process of digital appropriation. The concept of the remix is an analogue of the variability principle, and it has been applied to various creative fields, including the visual arts (Navas, 2018). The work of Jennifer Chan certainly relates to this process of remix. Her appropriation of references from a wide variety of sources speaks to the ability for post-digital artists to treat digital technologies such as the internet as just another resource from which to draw.

Jennifer Chan is a Canadian artist, writer, and curator who engages with and employs post-internet artistic practices. Beginning in 2011, she worked primarily in digital video-based works including GIF's and YouTube videos. These works addressed "gender and race politics in reaction to the media's promise of happiness."[6] In these video pieces, a wide variety of techniques and styles are combined in ways that are often jarring, and that reference an unskilled approach to video editing. Of these video works, Chan states: "Bad videomaking seemed sincere, effortless and convenient for the net. My older videos were inspired by fan culture on YouTube and could be lumped in with screen-recorded videos, unboxings, and reviews made by young videogamers" (Hirsch, 2014).

Her later work has combined digital video and interactive media with objects in installation-based works. For example, the work *Ally (Nice White*

Person) from 2018 which was featured in "Dude, Where's My Phallus?" curated by Kate Benedict at Bunker 2, Toronto is composed of a Moomin stuffed toy sitting on an IKEA stool, its back facing the viewer as the enter the space. The work has been altered as such; the plush toy wears a bracelet that reads "GOOD CSS" with a miniature cellphone dangling from the bracelet. Across the back of the toy reads RESPECT embroidered in varsity font. On the front chest of the Moomin is an embroidered white ribbon.

Moomins were created by Finnish author Tove Jansson in 1939 (Allerdice, 2019). Since the publication of the nine original Moomin children's book, they have become a worldwide phenomenon. In the title of this work we see the shift that Chan presents to the viewer. What might be a recognizable cartoon figure becomes a statement on identity, with the title referring to one who is not a part of a disenfranchised or oppressed group but supports the group from their own cultural position. The "Nice White Person" in this case might be the viewer of the piece, or it might be a reference to the Moomin character who could be an ally for Tove Jansson herself. Jansson was known to be bisexual and was in a committed relationship with a woman at a time when this was illegal in Finland (Shilling, 2017).

Another reference is made through the bracelet worn by the Moomin character. This bracelet contains a reference to coding practices. CSS stands for Cascading Style Sheets, and "Describes how HTML elements are to be displayed on screen, paper, or in other media."[7] The field of computer coding is dominated by white men, which makes another reference to the title of the piece. A further reference is the white ribbon embroidered on the chest of the Moomin. The white ribbon is, most likely, a reference to the White Ribbon Campaign, which was started in 1991 in London Ontario, as a response to male violence against women.[8]

In these alterations to the Moomin character, Chan loads the popular children's cartoon character with numerous references to popular culture. In this manner, she is continuing the digital video strategies of juxtaposition, but in a different medium. This type of approach is what makes her work representative of a post-internet approach to artmaking, which is similar to the concept of the post-digital. The main difference is that post-internet work is specific to the internet, while post-digital can be seen as more general in scope. Her work might be made of code, or it might be made of a store-bought plush toy. Regardless of the medium used, one can see similar strategies of appropriation and juxtaposition in her work. This is work that speaks to a cultural moment where networked digital technologies are ubiquitous, to the point where it does not seem that absurd that a plush toy would be wearing a charm bracelet that features a tiny cellphone.

The approaches used by post-internet artists are varied. This is not unique to artmaking, as artists have always borrowed from a variety of influences, and often combine media in a variety of ways. What makes post-internet artists unique is that the internet is treated as a medium. As Ceci Moss (2015) states: "Under the designation postinternet or internet aware, internet art was not required to be online, but rather referred to art enmeshed within an informational culture, online and off" (p. 155). In this enmeshment, the internet is not used as the principle medium, as in the work of previous net.artists such as Keith and Mendhi Obadike. It is a medium that can be combined with any number of media, historical or not.

In this way of working, the media can be seen as being decentralized. It becomes very challenging to describe the material aspects of the work, especially when the references are numerous and wide-ranging. The internet creates a flattening of previous cultural hierarchies and has also increased access to the means of production, as Chan describes in the previous quote. Poorly made YouTube videos exist alongside professionally produced works, and in work such as *Ally (Nice White Person)* (2018), references to computer coding, cartoon characters, and violence against women are all brought into the same rhizomatic set of connections.

The concepts of the post-digital and the remix both draw directly from music: the post-digital derives from electronic music and glitch, and the remix from hip hop. The remix in particular raises the issue of cultural appropriation. In writing about the work of remix artist Paul D. Miller, a.k.a. DJ Spooky That Subliminal Kid, Stewart (2010) scrutinizes the relationship between the theory of the remix, digital technologies, and cultural appropriation:

> Miller claims the history of African experience in America as a forerunner to DJ culture and the hyper-mediated contemporary world: the internet provides a globalized arena for people to inhabit multiple personas and avatars. In Miller's view, the history and legacy of slavery in America and the resulting forms of multiplex consciousness in African diasporic communities prepared those communities for this situation and for DJ cultures in which performers constantly speak through the recorded expressions of others (p. 356).

Provided with this reading of the remix, it is imperative that digital appropriation and cultural appropriation are continually scrutinized. "Simply to subsume hip hop under the slippery rubric of postmodernism is to run the risk of obscuring its origins in the African diaspora and its continuities with earlier Afrological forms" (p. 339). Stewart (2010) theorizes that postmodernism and "Afrological" artforms exist in simultaneity. Although "multiplex consciousness" predated the era of postmodernity, they can exist in parallel relationships with one another.

In the remix issues of ownership and fair use are brought to the fore. These are issues that are not directly addressed by Yoon, in *Eyes* (2018). However, by sharing the underlying "tools" that are used in the piece with the viewer, she opens the possibility that they could be used to recreate the work. These are issues that are continually being argued, both culturally and legally, with regard to digital technologies. My aim is not to digress further into these issues. I do want to acknowledge that references to the remix contained in this book, and to variability in general, in this book, are built upon mechanisms of cultural appropriation that should be questioned and critically examined. A Digital Visual Art Education must acknowledge the complexities of these issues, as they will undoubtedly continue to expand in the future, exacerbated by the availability of digital information and the digital divides that continue to exist. These are issues that often fade into the background of digitally networked daily life, as it is often assumed that these technologies are either entirely beneficial, or at the very least have a neutral impact on the user, and society in general. The combination of near-ubiquitous integration and proliferating ways to monitor and track individuals has led to expansive mechanisms of control that relate to the concept of intersectionality.

Interactivity

The third quality of digital visuality that I will be discussing in this book is interactivity. As stated by Mechant and Van Looy (2014): "In its most general sense, the term 'interactivity' describes an active relationship between at least two entities which can be people or object (p. 1)" At a general cultural level, relationships between people have been privileged over those between people and objects, or between objects and objects.[9]

Interactivity is a trait that is commonly associated with digital visual art in general, and specifically work that is based in the traditions of new media (Manovich, 2001). as well as interactive fiction and videogames. Digital visual artworks such as *My Hands Wishful Thinking* (2001) open up space for different forms of viewer interaction, as the net-based piece can be engaged with in any number of ways. Viewers can click on different areas of the image, which produce different visual and audio effects. New media art in this regard generally creates spaces for interactivity, in that the viewer can change visual and audio components of the piece in unique and idiosyncratic ways.

The relationship between interactivity and digital media has been well theorized. While many have found theories of interactivity to be useful in helping to understand the unique qualities of digital media, and digital visual art (Kwastek, 2015), others see in the term much that has yet to be defined and understood. Manovich (2001) discussed the relationship between interaction and new media art in detail, in The Language of New Media. However, in this book he also introduces the notion of "the myth of interactivity," in which he scrutinizes the choice-based interfaces that are a part of popular digital media such as DVD's as well as Interactive Fiction and videogames. Manovich is skeptical of the liberatory aspects that underly the rhetoric behind interactivity, seeing much of it as the user making choices that are determined by the programmer or designer.

Manovich addresses interactivity as related to digital media in general as such: "I still think that the interactivity remains the most difficult among the new cultural dimensions brought about by computerization—I still have not seen anybody developing any systematic theory of interactivity" (Quaranta, 2004, p. 30). I will certainly not propose such a theory here. Instead, I will look to theories of interactivity as they relate to modes of digital play found specifically in Interactive Fiction and videogames, with the hopes that the interactive elements of these experiences can provide art, design, and media educators with concepts that can allow for digital visual art to be better understood, produced, and received.

Of course, there are many works of digital visual art that minimize opportunities for interaction. One pertinent example here is a digital game called Cow Clicker, which was made by Ian Bogost in 2010. As Bogost (n.d.) states: "Cow Clicker" is a Facebook game about Facebook games. It's partly a satire, and partly a playable theory of today's social games, and partly an earnest example of that genre (n.p.). In Cow Clicker, you are given a cartoon cow that you can click. When you click your cow, you must wait six hours until you can click it again. Each time you click, you are provided with "mooney" that you can spend in the game to shorten the time between clicks.

Cow Clicker is interactive, in the basic sense of the term. However, what Cow Clicker presents is actually a constraint on interaction. After the first click, the cow does not respond, no matter how many times you click your cow. Bogost did not anticipate that this game would become popular, but her was proven wrong. At the height of it's popularity, it had 56,000 users on Facebook (Tanz, 2010). This popularity inspired Bogost to adapt the game so that it would eventually self-destruct in what he called the "Cowpocalypse." But before the game could self-destruct, Bogost embedded numerous critiques of the problems that he saw in numerous popular casual games. He developed the idea of clickification, which was a critique of the term gamification. He also embedded a sarcastic response to games that take part in clicktivism or donating to charitable causes through gameplay. His "Cow Clicktivism" cow raised 1,125 American dollars for Oxfam America (Tanz, 2010).

Here we see an absurdist digital game that speaks to serious issues in gaming communities, digital media development, and social media use. The limitations to interactivity that were built into Cow Clicker were intended as a critique of casual games, and perhaps videogames as a whole. However, the game became popular, either because of, or in spite of, the lack of choices made available to the player. Interactivity will be discussed in more detail in Chapter Five, as it can help us to better understand the possibilities as well as the limitations of a Digital Visual Art Education.

Intersectionality

The last quality of digital visual art that will inform the analyses that make up a Digital Visual Art Education is intersectionality. Intersectionality was first theorized by critical race theorist and black feminist legal scholar Kimberlé Crenshaw. In her landmark essay Demarginalizing the Intersection of Race and Sex: A Black Feminist Critique of Antidiscrimination Doctrine, Feminist Theory, and Antiracist Politics (1989), Crenshaw states the following:

> I argue that Black women are sometimes excluded from feminist theory and antiracist policy discourse because both are predicated on a discrete set of experiences that often does not accurately reflect the interaction of race and gender. These problems of exclusion cannot be solved simply by including Black women within an already established analytical structure. Because the intersectional experience is greater than the sum of racism and sexism, any analysis that does not take intersectionality into account cannot sufficiently address the particular manner in which Black women are subordinated. Thus, for feminist theory and antiracist policy discourse to embrace the experiences and concerns of Black women, the entire framework that has been used as a basis for translating "Women's experience" or "the Black experience" into concrete policy demands must be rethought and recast. (p. 140)

Because the theory of intersectionality informs much of what I propose in this book, I want to acknowledge the specific origins of this theory, as it has been applied in numerous fields since it originated in the field of legal studies. These widespread appropriations are not without controversy, prompting Crenshaw herself to speak to her original intent (Davis, 2019). I do not want to add to this somewhat problematic situation by claiming that decentralization is another form of intersectionality. My intent is comparing the two is simply to point to the complexities that intersectionality has identified in law, race, labor, and gender studies, and to suggest that digital visual art can present readings of sociocultural situations that are equally as complicated.

These complications have risen to a national level of scrutiny following the election of Donald Trump as President of the United States in 2016, and the social disruptions that have developed out of the COVID-19 global epidemic mentioned in the forward. Intersectionality plays a central role in the approaches to analyzing race and power known as Critical Race Theory (CRT). While CRT had been utilized in academia for decades, it was not until issues of race and power came to the forefront with the emergence of Black Lives Matter and the murder of George Floyd that it gained national notoriety. The relationship between these intersectional forms of influence and control is rooted in four hundred years of the US slave trade, the civil rights movement, and more recent forms of visuality where division is sown and examples of police brutality are broadcast to a worldwide audience. Intersectionality is a powerful theory, and researchers must always acknowledge the ways that legal theory and racial injustice create its foundation. Although it originated in the field of legal studies, it is a concept that can allow for productive complications of identity politics and power relationships (Aghasaleh, 2018). Here I will use the theory to analyze the work of Wanda Raimundi.

Wanda Raimundi is a "nationally and internationally recognized, award winning interdisciplinary visual and performance artist" (Raimundi, n.d.) She uses a variety of media and artistic strategies to make work that deals with cultural and ethnic identity. Her digital video performances use YouTube as a platform for pieces that speak to representation in the art world, through the performance persona Chuleta.[10] In seventeen separate *Ask Chuleta* (2005–present) video pieces, she comments upon current topics in the gallery-based contemporary art system, in the diaristic manner that most have come to associate with the weblog. As Raimundi writes:

> In the guise of my alter ego, Chuleta, a sassy, no-nonsense NuyoRican art enthusiast became my way of calling out biases of both the art world as well as my own people by becoming a sort of urban art translator, conduit, culture critic, interceptor and interrogator. It was a wild experiment that predates current YouTube styling and confessional style video format designed to breach the art world and reach out beyond the confines of the "white cube" to talk to anyone that wanted to listen (n.d.).

In the *Ask Chuleta #6: Identity Art* video from 2011, Raimundi presents an analysis of herself through her Chuleta persona: "She be doing performance art, and she be doing murals… she's like a jack-of-all-trades. And that makes me mad excited because, you know, you don't have to be doing just one thing. You can do all different stuff." This self-reflexivity allows Raimundi to reflect upon serious conditions in the contemporary gallery-based art market using satire. This video speaks to identity art and identity politics. In character, she makes reference to contemporary performance artists William Pope L., and Dread Scott, making the point that oftentimes performance art is used to agitate and provoke. She ends the video by speaking to gender representation in contemporary performance art, stating that "Usually it's dudes that are doing that shit."

Her 2017 piece titled *Pieta* was performed in the Smithsonian National Portrait gallery. As she writes: "My live performance is a multi-sensory durational piece where I examine the ever present fear of losing a child to violence as a woman of color and a mother to a small brown boy" (n.p.). Raimundi sat in the National Portrait Gallery, dressed in a manner that referenced Michelangeo's *Pieta* (1498–1499). Further referencing this work, she invited 33 persons of color to the stage, where the cradled them for three minutes and thirty-three seconds. As Raimundi states, this number is "a nod to the age that Jesus Christ was at the time of his execution" (n.p.). In an interview dealing with the piece, Raimundi states the following: "I started thinking about things that make me anxious, started thinking about my son, thinking about examining my own experiences with injustice, and my own privileges of having fair skin" (UCF). This last comment speaks to the way that the concept of intersectionality is currently being used to better understand the complex relationship between race, identity, and privilege.

Interconnectedness, indeterminacy, interactivity, and intersectionality as I have been describing them are certainly not unique to the field of digital visual art. Digital visual art, however, might be the best way to observe the complexities of contemporary issues such as gender, race, power, and commerce. In the examples that I have discussed, the Obadike's, Chan, and

Raimundi are each speaking from positions that are traditionally marginalized in the contemporary gallery/museum-based artworld. An intersectional reading of these forms of marginalization as theorized by Crenshaw would take into account race and gender as related to the institutional structures within which they operate. However, for Crenshaw, the emphasis upon Black women as doubly marginalized is important to point out. This would apply to Mendhi Obadike specifically. Chan and Raimundi can be seen as relating to this framework, but as women of Puerto Rican and Korean descent, the extent to which they are marginalized would generally be considered less than one who identifies as being Black (Although this is certainly debatable as it depends upon a multitude of additional factors such as socioeconomic class, sexuality, and disability to name a few).

In the framework of their digital visual works of art, these intersectional identities are exaggerated, questioned, and generally problematized. The blunt measurements that apply in the legal argument of Crenshaw are not so easily rendered when discussing the work of the Obadike's, Chan, and Raimundi. This is what digital visual art can provide, and what legal doctrine generally hopes to avoid; digital visual art can incorporate simultaneous, incomplete, and often contradictory identity formations. Digital visual art can present the paradoxical, while it also speaks to underlying problematics. Digital visual art can exist between the poles of binary social arrangements and can occupy spaces between the nodes of a digital visual identity. Intersectionality can help to analyze the complex social and cultural relationships that generate power or that lead to the lack thereof. Intersectionality aligns with my previous discussions of decentralized networks as they relate to digital visual works of art, primarily in the way that it maps power relationships as being dynamic and interconnected. The intersectional aspects of Raimundi's work are primarily focused on identity as it relates to race, class, and gender. Through her performative explorations, she decenters her own artistic authority, first working through her alter ego Chuleta, and then presenting herself as various generalized persona: queen, mother, Virgin Mary. Her strategy of decentralizing her artistic identity is one that is amplified by her use of digital media. As anyone familiar with contemporary social media are well-aware, the opportunities for self-representation on these platforms are numerous. However, as Raimundi reminds us, visual art has always offered the viewer the opportunity to see themselves in a different light. This might be accomplished by borrowing from the visual language of YouTube videos, or from European Renaissance sculpture. As Jennifer Chan reminds us, the internet is a medium that can be used as a mirror, to reflect aspects of our identities back to us.

In these four examples of digital visual artistic practices, we can see that interconnectedness, indeterminacy, interaction, and intersectionality are relevant in distinct ways. In the practices of Keith and Mendhi Obadike, we see a decentralized work of art. The manifold versions of a work of art such as *My Hands Wishful Thinking* (2001) speaks to the challenges of isolating a single, complete work of art. With Jennifer Chan, we see post-internet practices that result in a decentralized, post-digital use of media forms. In *Ally (Nice White Person)* (2018) the modified plush Moomin figure channels references to race, computer code, and violence against women, taking her previous approach to working in digital video and applying it in sculptural form. In Cow Clicker (2010) by Ian Bogost, we see opportunities for interaction enclosed upon, with humorous and serious results. And in *Ask Chuleta* (2005–present) by Wanda Raimundi, we see a decentralized, open-ended form of artistic identity. Her work speaks to race, class, and gender in an intersectional manner, which is extended and expanded through her use of post-digital media.

Digital Visuality and Dataveillance

An analysis of digital visual works of art through this developing theory of digital visuality and the constituent elements of interconnectedness, indeterminacy, interactivity, and intersectionality can help to provide the framework for a Digital Visual Art Education. This is a form of analysis that foregrounds discussions of identity, materiality, and power. In order to further explore these topics, I will now look to theories of surveillance as they take place within networked digital technologies. Surveillance consists of multiple sociocultural elements and apparatuses that are based in visuality, and the aspect that I will therefore be using to expand the theory of digital visuality is dataveillance.

The term dataveillance was first used by Clarke (1988) who defined it as such: "Dataveillance is the systematic use of personal data systems in the investigation or monitoring of the actions or communications of one or more persons" (n.p.). This systematic use of data has seen exponential growth since the time that these words were written, seeing both the rise of "big data" as well as movements such as "The Quantified Self." (Barry, 2020). In fact, Mitchell (2012) argues that the contemporary masses of data combined with innovations in biotechnology have given rise to a condition of "uberveillance."[11]

In dataveillance, the primacy of visuality in traditional surveillance methods are supplanted by digital information. Yoon speaks to this topic in reference to her work as such:

> In this digital era, the main problems with the use of biometric data are the misuse of personal data and privacy issues since the data contains information acquired from individuals. Sometimes, biometric data can be stolen for other purposes or crimes, which is a source of great concern in society. Although people are afraid of having their biometric data stolen, the use of biometric data is becoming more commonplace in this era due to the ease and convenience it offers as a method of verifying an individual's identity. As more digital applications request people to input their biometric data as a more convenient and secure method of identification, the possibility of losing their personal data and identities may increase (n.p.).

This statement speaks to a binary relationship between biometrics and dataveillance. In this dualistic description personal data can be stolen, but this is countered by the ease and convenience that it provides. I suggest that the situation described is perhaps not so equally balanced. Of course, personal information can be stolen by hackers and thieves, but it is far more common for individuals to offer up their own personal information voluntarily, whether on social media, through email, or over the telephone. The ability to monitor the behavior of an individual user is not unique to contemporary networked digital technologies. Paul Baran, in fact, wrote about this issue not long after his work on distributed communications:

> Back in 1968, he published an article explaining how the collection of personal data threatens individual autonomy and can bring societal problems that might be impossible to overcome (displaying his trademark wit, Baran also joked, for example, that the availability of dental records would betray those of our friends whose teeth were not their own). His answer to the problem involved more than just concentrating on practical solutions (although he was active on that front as well, and in 1965 he invented an end-to-end message encryption method which led to the creation of today's encrypted communicators like Signal and WhatsApp). He believed that engineers should take responsibility for their inventions and address privacy and other ethical and social concerns at the level of design, ensuring that new technologies did not bring unplanned problems, but made them preventable (Wieczorek, 2020, n.p.).

While Baran identified the technical aspects of dataveillance and digital security in the early days of the internet, he was not as concerned with the social aspects of these issues. Approaching these issues from a philosophical perspective, Gilles Deleuze (1992) described this situation in his essay titled

Postscripts on the Societies of Control. In this essay, Deleuze builds upon the work of Michel Foucault, who spoke to the parameters of disciplinary societies and the control that they exert over the individual in Discipline and Punish: The Birth of the Prison (1975). For Deleuze, the enclosures that Foucault analyzes are in a state of upheaval, particularly after World War II:

> We are in a generalized crisis in relation to all the environments of enclosure—prison, hospital, factory, school, family. The family is an "interior," in crisis like all other interiors—scholarly, professional, etc. The administrations in charge never cease announcing supposedly necessary reforms: to reform schools, to reform industries, hospitals, the armed forces, prisons. But everyone knows that these institutions are finished, whatever the length of their expiration periods. It's only a matter of administering their last rites and of keeping people employed until the installation of the new forces knocking at the door.

The disciplinary societies have led to societies of control, which exert power over its subjects not through distinct systems, but through continual modulation:

> In the societies of control, on the other hand, what is important is no longer either a signature or a number, but a code: the code is a password, while on the other hand the disciplinary societies are regulated by watchwords (as much from the point of view of integration as from that of resistance). The numerical language of control is made of codes that mark access to information, or reject it. We no longer find ourselves dealing with the mass/individual pair. Individuals have become "dividuals," and masses, samples, data, markets, or "banks."

I will be discussing the notion of the "dividual" as it relates to identity in a Digital Visual Art Education later in the book in Chapter Four. For the current discussion of digital visuality, it is important to scrutinize the emphasis Deleuze places on code in the previous passage. The code determines access, but in the process of becoming a dividual, the subject is fragmented, becoming the code. Here, the reference to optical scanning in *Eyes* (2018) is relevant. The information that the iris provides is not a code that can be memorized, falsified, or forgotten. It is embodied, and just like fingerprints or DNA for that matter, it is thought to be unique to that person.

Eyes (2018) can therefore be understood as a statement on code: the code that is provided by the body, to the computer, which is translated into various forms, to be read again by the body, and on and on. I have suggested previously that new media artists are uniquely positioned to speak to the dysfunctional aspects of digital technology, as they can set into motion feedback loops such as the one described in this work. This process of iteration is not part of the scientific method, as most new media artists do not work through the formal process of testing hypotheses, gathering data, and making conclusions based on this process. They offer multiple possibilities simultaneously, much in the way that Yoon's work is displayed in three manifestations. Interestingly, she speaks to this process in her artist statement for the work:

> The questions of identification and the insecurity of biometric data have become my inspiration, providing artistic approaches to the manipulation of biometric data and having the potential to suggest new directions for solving the problems.

While I can understand the urge to want to solve problems such as these, I am convinced that digital visual art may also contribute to the problem, through the obfuscation of the issues at hand, or the fetishization of the technologies that can be used to track and control. These are issues that must be addressed through a Digital Visual Art Education. Digital Visual Art Education can make use of the theory of digital visuality through the paired concepts of interconnection and reflexivity, indeterminacy and variability, interactivity and play, and intersectionality and power. These concepts will now be applied to the work of Hasan Elahi, to suggest approaches for artists, educators, and theorists who are making, teaching from, and researching digital visual works of art.

Hasan Elahi is a digital visual artist whose work relates directly to the issues of digital visuality that I have been discussing in this chapter. As he states on his website: "Hasan Elahi is an artist whose work examines issues of surveillance, citizenship, migration, transport, and the challenges of borders and frontiers" (2020, n.p.). His work titled Tracking Transience (2003-present) is perhaps the work that can best speak to the concept of decentralized visuality. *Tracking Transience* (http://www.trackingtransience.com) started when Elahi was detained by the FBI as he was returning from an overseas trip in June of 2002. Following this encounter, and subsequent interrogations where he was given a Polygraph test, it was recommended that Elahi reach out to the FBI if he "got into any trouble" (2011). Elahi took this invitation and expanded upon it, calling the FBI with detailed travel information. This led to him emailing the FBI with detailed travel information, a process which eventually he automated by creating a website that would post his current location using digital photographs and GPS data. This project became *Tracking Transience.*

Tracking Transience (2003-present) is a website that opens with a horizontally split-screen. The top half shows a photograph that is scrolling, while the bottom half shows a GPS satellite image, with a large red arrow indicating Elahi's current location. The site also includes a pop-up message from Google, which appears to be in Chinese, and the words "for development purposes only" repeated across the map image. There are also a number of small black squares with a red drop shadow across the center of the page. Clicking on these squares changes the GPS satellite image but provides no further information. This home screen is displayed for 30 seconds before it is replaced by a slide show of sorts: photographs of airports and food served on airplanes, documentation of food purchased in grocery stores, and bank records that show these purchases, and images of airport bathrooms and hotel rooms. The site contained over 70,000 images as of May 2016 (Artsy, 2016), and has continued to grow as Elahi continues to travel.

Tracking Transience (2003–present) is a multilayered work that touches upon numerous important social issues. The first issue that should be discussed as related to decentralized visuality is the way that the work addresses visibility. As a Bangladeshi-born American person, he is subject to additional scrutiny due to his skin color and perceived religious affiliation, as indicated by his initial detainment by the FBI in 2002, soon after September 11, 2001. It is clear that Elahi is making a statement on surveillance and monitoring through this incessant visual documentation. In making so many aspects of his life visible to the viewer of the work, one might think that Elahi is giving up his freedom. However, he speaks to this issue as follows:

> I still stand behind the idea that you protect your privacy by giving it up, but I also acknowledge that even in the years I've been tracking myself, our culture and opinions of surveillance have changed. When I first started this project and my friends found out what I was doing, several of them told me not to show up at their house. These days, they hardly even notice their smartphones are tracking them much more accurately than I ever could. (Elahi, 2011)

The documentation that Elahi started to gather following his detainment by the FBI might have seemed invasive when he started in 2003. However, the tracking capabilities of contemporary smartphones combined with the ubiquity of social media has made his practices seem less so.

The visibility that Elahi builds into *Tracking Transience* (2003–present) is somewhat different from that discussed earlier in the work of Yoon Chung Han. Elahi is making visual documentation of his daily activities, while Yoon makes visible the tools used to create her work. As works of digital visual art, both make use of code that helps to structure the work. Elahi's website clearly uses Google Maps to track his movement. This acknowledgement is a nod to the prevalence of GPS satellite technologies and their ability to provide a comprehensive view on almost every part of the globe. As such, both works speak to aspects of vision and visuality.

Both works speak to vision as it takes place within and through networked digital technologies. They are both reflexive, but in different ways. Yoon's *Eyes* (2018) uses the digital image of the eye of the viewer to speak to issues of data visualization and biometrics. Elahi's *Tracking Transience* (2003–present) uses the digital photograph and GPS satellite imagery to speak to how networked digital technologies influence how we see, and how we are seen. In a similar manner, Elahi's work *Retina* (2018), installed at Bard College, makes use of variability. This work is, perhaps, closer to Yoon's *Eyes* (2018) than *Tracking Transience* (2003–present), when discussing formal qualities. *Retina* (2018) is a 64 foot long photographic reproduction of a Google Street View image of the scene across from the building. In reproducing the work upside down and in black and white, Elahi is making a reference to the physiological act of seeing. He is also, at the same time, speaking to the visuality that is enabled by current networked digital technologies. In an interview that was conducted as part of the installation of this work, Elahi states:

> In considering surveillance we tend to think of it as a very 21st century concept, yet we've always been watched. We've had several thousands of years of being watched from above; G-d—all knowing—as the original surveillance camera. This might sound sarcastic, but there's a very similar omniscience that a lot of these data companies have about us. I think we don't consider many things as surveillance until it's put in that context for us. Similarly, when you hyper aestheticize an image your brain no longer reads it as surveillance, but reads it as landscape and I think there's something that also happens when you take that Google Street View image and you aestheticize it. (2018).

In the model of the decentralized network, we understand how the flow of information can be improved through feedback loops that relay data regarding efficiency and speed. In digital visual works of art, the feedback loops that are created through reflexive visual references and modes of interaction can just as easily demonstrate how the flow of information can be made dysfunctional. In *Eyes* (2018), the digital image of the eye of the viewer is made into data visualization as well as sound, which speaks to the aspects of contemporary life that are beyond the apprehension of the eye. In *Tracking Transience* (2003–present), the flow of information is overwhelming, serving as a comprehensive record of Elahi's travels but also making it very challenging to find specific information. As he states: "Actually when you go to my site, the interface is not very user-friendly. It's actually user unfriendly. Everything is there, but you have to really work through it." (2011).

It is in the work of digital visual artists that the model of the decentralized network speaks to various levels of function and dysfunction. As I have previously argued, digital visual artists are in a unique position to be able to highlight dysfunctional aspects of networked digital technologies. Here I argue that by focusing on decentralized visuality, digital visual artists can challenge the notion that vision is natural, in the manner that Haraway (2001) identifies. Doing this through visual means opens up further questions and complicates previously clear points of view.

The use of accessible technological tools by Elahi and Yoon provides openings for their works to be reworked, rethought, and remixed, which leads to the third aspect of digital visuality: variability. The variable nature of *Eyes* (2018) can be seen in the different ways that the work can be presented to the viewer, in both gallery and online settings. *Tracking Transience* (2003–present) is also a work that uses variability in important ways. It exists as a website, but it has also been presented in site specific installations in various locations. When displayed in gallery setting, the work is typically shown through photographic reproductions of the web-based documentary photos. These reproductions allow the works to be shown in a variety of groupings, which amplifies the relationships between them, and allows for them to be categorized.

Last, we should consider the ways that these works relate to dataveillance. As previously discussed, Yoon states that *Eyes* (2018) is a work that is concerned with biometric data and identity. This is a form of monitoring that uses the eye to scan and screen, combining both visual information and data. Dataveillance is perhaps the most prominent feature of *Tracking Transience* (2013–present), seen in the content of the work and the many statements by Elahi. However, the process that he sets in motion shifts the fixed relationship between observer and observed. As Elahi states:

> This was before people were Tweeting everywhere and 750 million were posting status messages or poking people. I'm glad that this is obsolete. We are creating our own archives. And one of the things that I do is look through my server logs very carefully, because it's about surveillance. I'm watching who's watching me. (2012)

As stated earlier, *Tracking Transience* (2003–present) predated the current use of social media. The ability for Elahi to watch who is watching through the creation of this database relates to the concept of sousveillance, or a view from below. Sousveillance has been presented as a form of resistance to overreaching surveillance technologies and ideologies and is relevant when discussing decentralized visuality and the power related to seeing and being seen.

Art, design, and media educators who are engaged with digital visual works of art must take into consideration the ways that such works speak to and enable a variety of forms of visuality. This digital visuality works with notions of the visible, as both image and as computer code, referencing the tools that are used to make the work. It works in a reflexive manner, speaking to human sight as biological and social. It introduces a level of variability, where the work can be reconfigured and revised. And last, it draws upon the dynamic power structures found in contemporary surveillance and dataveillance, where technologies of seeing and being seen are fused with massive amounts of digital information.

To review: the four basic concepts that I will use to inform my approach to Digital Visual Art Education are interconnectedness, indeterminateness, interactivity, and intersectionality. While my focus will be digital visual art, there will be moments where these concepts can be applied to examples from related areas and fields. For example, these concepts can help us to better understand the shifts in educational systems that were mentioned in my forward. With regards to decentralization, the traditional classroom models, as varied as they are across the US, nevertheless maintain a certain level of centralization. Physical centralization, in the form of students in desks in the same space; Curricular centralization, in the form of a shared schedule and set of information that is to be learned; Pedagogical centralization, in the form of a teacher that organizes and manages the curriculum, and a hierarchical power structure within schools and districts.

The COVID-19 global pandemic is forcing these models to shift, at a scale that is unprecedented. While there have been small forays into distance learning as the technologies have become more familiar and widespread, and as cyberschools have entered into the mainstream, there has not been change at this scale since, perhaps, the Industrial Revolution. Speculation aside, our current moment is bringing about change on a global scale. While much of this change will take time to discern, we can attend to the changes that are on the horizon for public education in the US as they relate to decentralized communicational models. There have been numerous attempts to reform educational systems throughout the 19th and 20th centuries. Previous attempts to introduce decentralized forms of education, such as the Open Classroom Movement, were not successful for a variety of reasons. In the 21st century, we now confront unprecedented social and cultural shifts. Prior to the COVID-19 global pandemic, 21% of public schools offered at least one class online.[12] As the 2020–2021 school year begins, we see 20 of the 25 largest school systems in the country shifting to exclusive online instruction.[13]

If we look at this situation through the model of the decentralized network, we might be able to see a way to diagram these shifting relationships between learner, teacher, administrator, staff member, and family member. However, this only goes so far. The diagram of the decentralized network can provide a way to understand the complex communicational forms that take place within a given system, but this diagram does not tell us much beyond that. For more instructions, we can turn to artists who use these networks, artists who creatively and critically assess these networks. Contemporary art can speak to contemporary issues in a direct manner, as Hausman (1963) argued. And it is artists that Deleuze and Guattari (1987) single out, after all, for their capacities to make maps and not tracings.

These are an example of the aspects of Digital Visual Art Education that I will be presenting in the chapters to follow. Through each chapter, I will apply these concepts in the analysis of topics such as digital virality and data visualization, post-digital materiality and makerspaces; interactive fiction and videogames; and digital visual identity and digital video. Although decentralization, incompleteness, and the post-digital will inform the chapters that follow, I want to resist the urge to apply these concepts in a universal manner. There are certainly digital visual works of art that reflect a centralized structure, just as there are those that are distributed. There are digital visual works of art that might be seen as quite complete, more arborescent than rhizomatic. And there are, of course, digital visual works of art that are defiantly not post-digital. As I have shown in the previous examples, these concepts can allow art educators to better understand, and therefore better teach from some of the more challenging aspects of contemporary digital visual works of art.

Notes

1 D3 stands for Data-Driven Document, and is used for data visualization (https://d3js.org). Three is a program that allows 3D computer graphics to be displayed in a web browser (https://threejs.org). Max/MSP is a program that is used to create interactive sounds and graphics (https://cycling74.com).

2 As I mentioned in the introduction, net.art is a specific category of digital visual art that is quite relevant to the development of a Digital Visual Art Education, as net.art was

initially made on the internet, and was intended to be distributed within these electronic communicational networks.

3 See Sweeny, R. (2017). Dysfunction and Decentralization in New Media Art and Education for an in-depth analysis of the history of electronic communication and its relationship to digital visual art.

4 This piece can be viewed at https://obadike.squarespace.com/#/ice/

5 The emergence of Non-Fungible Tokens has shifted this quality somewhat dramatically. NFT's will be discussed later in this book in Chapter Three.

6 http://front.bc.ca/events/jennifer-chan-2/

7 https://www.w3schools.com/css/css_intro.asp

8 https://en.wikipedia.org/wiki/White_Ribbon_Campaign

9 In Chapter Four I will discuss the field of Feminist New Materialsm and Actor-Network Theory, which both aim to scrutinize and dismantle these forms of privileging.

10 https://www.raimundiart.com

11 "In layman terms, uberveillance is a kind of CCTV on the 'inside' looking out rather than on the 'outside' looking down: an 'above and beyond', an exaggerated 24/7 surveillance embedded inside the human body. Locating, tracking, and real-time monitoring without any cease, that is, constant and unending." (n.p.).

12 https://nces.ed.gov/fastfacts/display.asp?id=79

13 As of August 18 2020, 20 of the 25 largest school districts are choosing remote learning only as their back-to-school instructional model, affecting over 4.3 million students. https://www.edweek.org/ew/section/multimedia/school-districts-reopening-plans-a-snapshot.html?_ga=2.156766076.630882968.1598018207-419876066.1598018207

References

Aghasaleh, R. (2018). Oppressive Curriculum: Sexist, Racist, Classist, and Homophobic Practice of Dress Codes in Schooling. *Journal of African American Studies*, *22*(1), 94–108. http://www.jstor.org/stable/45200244

Allardice, L. (2019). 'It is a religion': How the World Went Mad for Moomin. *The Guardian*. Retrieved March 2023 from https://www.theguardian.com/books/2019/apr/06/it-is-a-religion-how-the-world-went-mad-for-moomins

Artsy. (2016). *Hasan Elahi vs. The FBI: The Art of Self-Surveillance*. Retrieved March, 2023, from https://www.artsy.net/article/artsy-hasan-elahi-vs-the-fbi-the-art-of-self-surveillance

Baran, P. (1964). On Distributed Communications Networks. *IEEE Transactions of the Professional Technical Group on Communication Systems*, *CS-12*(1). RAND Corporation.

Barry, L. (2020). The Quantified Self and the Digital Making of the Subject. In M. Stocchetti (Ed.), *The Digital Age and Its Discontents: Critical Reflections in Education* (pp. 95–110). Helsinki Univers.

Bogost, I. (n.d.). *Cow Clicker*. Retrieved February, 2023, from https://bogost.com/games/cow_clicker/ ity Press.

Bookchin, N., & Shulgin, A. (1999). *Introduction to net.art* (work of art).

Bryson, N. (1988). The Gaze in the Expanded Field. In H. Foster (Ed.), *Vision and Visuality* (pp. 91–94). Seattle, WA: Bay View Press/Dia Art Foundation.

Cascone, K. (2000). The Aesthetics of Failure: 'Post-Digital' Tendencies in Contemporary Computer Music. *Computer Music Journal*, 24(4), 12–18. http://www.jstor.org/stable/3681551

Castells, M. (1996). *The Rise of the Network Society*. Wiley Blackwell.

Clarke, R. (1988). Information Technology and Dataveillance. *Communication of the* ACM *31*(5), 498–512.

Cole, T. (2015). A Visual Remix. *New York Times Magazine*. Accessed from https://www.nytimes.com/2015/04/19/magazine/a-visual-remix.html

Cramer, F. (2014). What Is 'Post-digital?' *APRJA*, 3(1).

Crenshaw, K. (1989). Demarginalizing the Intersection of Race and Sex: Black Feminist Critique of Antidiscrimination Doctrine, Feminist Theory and Antiracist Politics. *University of Chicago Legal Forum, 1989*, 139–168.

Davis, K. (2019). Who Owns Intersectionality? Some Reflections on Feminist Debates on How Theories Travel. *European Journal of Women's Studies*. https://doi.org/10.1177/1350506819892659

Deleuze, G., & Guattari, F. (1987). *A Thousand Plateaus*. University of Minnesota Press.

Deleuze, G. (1992, October). *Postscript on the Societies of Control* (pp. 3–7), 59. MIT Press.

DePriest, D. (2018/2019, Fall/Winter). Human Perceptual Changes in a Technological World—An Exploration. *C2C Digital Magazine*, p. 9.

Elahi, H. (2011). *I Share Everything. Or Do I?* Retrieved March, 2023 from: https://ideas.ted.com/i-share-everything-or-do-i/

Elkins, J. (2003). *Visual Studies: A Skeptical Introduction*. Routledge.

Foucault, M. (1975). *Discipline and Punish: The Birth of the Prison*. Random House.

Haraway, D. (2001). The Persistence of Vision. In Mirzoeff, N. (Ed.), *The Visual Culture Reader* (pp. 677–685). London: Routledge.

Hausman, J. (1963). Contemporary Art and Art Education. *Studies in Art Education*, 5(1), 82–91. https://doi.org/10.2307/1319992

Hirsch, A. (2014). *Artist Profile: Jennifer Chan*. Retrieved March, 2023, from https://rhizome.org/editorial/2014/dec/18/artist-profile-jennifer-chan/

Johnson, S. (2001). *Emergence: The Connected Lives of Ants, Brains, Cities, and Software*. Scribner.

Knustad, M. (n.d.). *Keith Obadike*. ELMCIP. Retrieved February, 2023, from https://elmcip.net/person/keith-obadike

Kwastek, K. (2015). *Aesthetics of Interaction in Digital Art*. MIT Press.

Lupton, D., & Williamson, B. (2017). The Datafied Child: The Dataveillance of Children and Implications for Their Rights. *New Media & Society*. Accessed from http://journals.sagepub.com/doi/full/10.1177/1461444816686328

Manovich, L. (2001). *The Language of New Media*. MIT Press.

Mechant & Van Looy. (2014). Interactivity. In M. L. Ryan, L. Emerson, & B. Robertson (Eds.), *The Johns Hopkins Guide to Digital Media*. Johns Hopkins University Press.

Mirzoeff, N. (Ed.) (1998). *The Visual Culture Reader*. Routledge.

Mirzoeff, N. (2011). The Right to Look. *Critical Inquiry*, *37*(3), 473–496. https://doi.org/10.1086/659354

Mitchell, M. (2012). *On the 'birth' of Uberveillance.* Retrieved March, 2023, from: http://uberveillance.com/blog/2012/2/15/on-the-birth-of-uberveillance.html

Moss, C. (2015). Internet Explorers. In L. Cornell & E. Halter (Eds.), *Mass Effect: Art and the Internet in the 21st Century*. MIT Press.

Navas, E. (2018). *Art, Media Design, and Postproduction. Open Guidelines on Appropriation and Remix*. Routledge

Obadike, K. (n.d.). *Mendhi and Keith Obadike.* Retrieved March, 2023, from: https://obadike.squarespace.com/#/ice/

Paul, C. (2020). *Histories of the Digital Now.* Retrieved March, 2023, from: https://whitney.org/essays/histories-of-the-digital-now

Quaranta, D. (2004). What Kind of Interaction? Interview with Lev Manovich. *Cluster. On Innovation*, no. 3 (Interaction Design), pp. 30–33.

Raimundi, W. (n.d.). *Wanda Raimundi.* Retrieved March, 2023, from https://www.raimundiart.com

Sharon, T., & Zandberg, D. (2016). From Data Fetishism to Quantifying Selves: Self-Tracking Practices and the Other Values of Data. *New Media & Society 2017*, *19*(11), 1695–1709. https://doi.org/10.1177/1461444816636090

Shilling, J. (2017). The Dark Side of the Moonins. *Prospect Magazine*. Retrieved from https://www.prospectmagazine.co.uk/magazine/the-dark-side-of-the-moomins

Stewart, J. (2010). DJ Spooky and the Politics of Afro-Postmodernism. *Black Music Research Journal*, 30(2), 337–362. Center for Black Music Research Columbia College Chicago and University of Illinois Press.

Sweeny, R. (2015). *Dysfunction and Decentralization in New Media Art and Education*. London, UK: Intellect Press.

Tanz, J. (2011). The Curse of Cow Clicker: How a Cheeky Satire Became a Videogame Hit. *Wired Magazine*. Retrieved February, 2023, from https://www.wired.com/2011/12/ff-cowclicker/

Varma, J. R. (1992 Autumn). Computer Graphics, Peripheral Vision and Non-Euclidian Geometry. *Computers & Graphics*, *16*(3), 253–258.

Wieczorek, M. (2020). *Averting the Apocalypse with Hot Potatoes: How Paul Baran Invented the Internet*. *Culture*. Retrieved March, 2023, from: https://culture.pl/en/article/how-paul-baran-invented-the-internet

· 2 ·

INTERCONNECTED: DIGITAL VIRALITY AND DATA VISUALIZATION

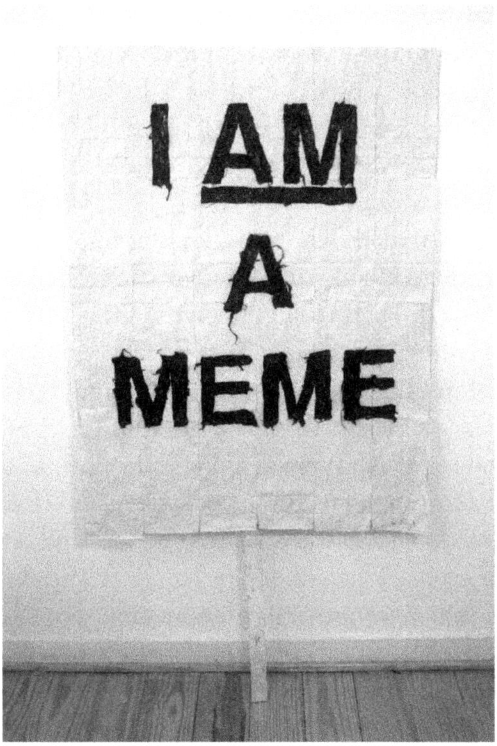

Figure 2.1. *How Can You Love Me and Hate Me at the Same Time?* (2011) Nathaniel Donnett. Paper bags, plastic, gold leaf foil, wood

Source: https://medium.com/@atbq6b/black-art-and-new-media-97d5cbd346c9 [accessed 8/16/2023]. Used with permission of the artist.

As referenced in the introductory image, there is a complicated relationship between identity and social media in many examples of contemporary art. The introductory image by Nathaniel Donnett (2011) depicts a sculptural object that references the "I AM A MAN" protest signs that were held by African American men in the 1968 Memphis sanitation strike.[1] In the Donnett work, "MAN" is replaced by "MEME." The piece is rather simple in terms of its presentation, but the references that it makes are dense. A detailed analysis of the work can help to better understand the impact that interconnected works of digital art can have within a Digital Visual Art Education.

First, I will analyze the work in terms of digital visuality. As I proposed in the first chapter, a digital visuality relies upon the concepts of interconnectedness and reflexivity. If we begin with the phrase that is written on the piece, we can already see a reflexive reference. "I AM A MEME." But who is "I?" In the 1968 protests, it was assumed that this reference was to the person holding the sign. Here, no one hold the sign. Is the "I" Nathaniel Donnett? Is it the viewer? Is it the sign itself? We will leave these questions unanswered for the time being; each response takes us in a different direction, which will be followed later in this chapter.

The next question that should be asked is as follows: What does it mean to be a meme? The concept of the meme comes from the work of Evolutionary Biologist Richard Dawkins, who first conceived of the term as a way to describe the transmission of culture in his book The Selfish Gene (1976). In this initial theory, Dawkins did not highlight the role that digital technologies played in the spread of memes. As he states: "…the internet uses just one tiny example of a meme. A meme is a much more general concept than that. But the internet is a very fertile ecosystem for the spread of memes" (Fazal, 2018, n.p.)

The internet makes visible the ways that images and text are adapted and spread, and digital technologies that are based in variability allow for this to happen in ways that were previously impossible. So, to be a meme means that, on a superficial level, aspects of your identity are shared on social media. Writing about *How Can You Love Me and Hate Me at the Same Time?* (2011), Martine Syms (2015) suggests the following: "Expressing pride at being a meme means establishing a link between personhood and the representation of a person" (p. 372). This is a profound statement. To be a meme, which is equated with being a passing fad, is seen by Syms as a foundational part of identity. Could it be that to be a person in the 21st century is to embrace the superficial, banal, and oftentimes odious aspects of social media?

In a 2015 essay, Syms writes about the piece as such:

> The original phrasing is appropriated and adapted to make a wry point about the formation of a black personhood within new media. The title is suggestive of a DuBosian twoness. The color line has birthed the digital divide, another mythic border that shadows our work. (p. 373)

Here identity is specified: The I is clearly a Black I, but identity in this case is divided along the lines of the double consciousness that W.E.B. DuBois (1903) famously described as such:

> It is a peculiar sensation, this double-consciousness, this sense of always looking at one's self through the eyes of others, of measuring one's soul by the tape of a world that looks on in amused contempt and pity. One ever feels his twoness,—an American, a Negro; two souls, two thoughts, two unreconciled strivings; two warring ideals in one dark body, whose dogged strength alone keeps it from being torn asunder (p. 38).

Syms' makes reference to Black personhood within new media. Here, the space of digital media production is just as divided as previous forms of personhood, even though early descriptions of digital social spaces such as the internet promised a utopian experience that would be free from historical forms of prejudice and bias. The term Digital blackface has been offered as a way to understand the contemporary appropriation of Black culture in social media (Abreu, n.d.). Digital blackface operates on two levels. The first level is simple cultural appropriation: the most used GIF's to communicate. The second level is perhaps more subtle. These reaction GIF's emphasize excessive emotional reactions to situations, which further reinforces the stereotype that Black people are more prone to fits of moodiness, anger, and violence (Jackson, 2013). As these memes circulate, these stereotypes become normalized, and in their intended humor and superficiality they gain additional cultural traction. They become a feedback loop that modulates behavior, especially with Black viewers who are the subject of the memes.

So what does it mean to be a Black meme? Here I will turn to the work of Legacy Russell, in order to explore this specific question, and to expand the conversation regarding memes in a Digital Visual Art Education. As it states on her personal webpage, Russell is a curator, writer, and artist: "Her academic, curatorial, and creative work focuses on gender, performance, digital selfdom, internet idolatry, and new media ritual." (Russell, n.d.). Much of her work deals with the intersections of race, gender, and digital technologies. Her work Black Meme (2020) is particularly relevant to the discussion of memes in digital visual culture.

In her artist statement for the work, Russell writes:

> BLACK MEME explores the construct, culture, and material of the "meme" as mapped to black visual culture from 1900 to present day. Using archival media Russell explores the impact of blackness, black life, and black social death on contemporary conceptions of virality borne in the age of the Internet (n.p.).

Black Meme (2020) is a video essay that begins with a screenshot of a user entering a phrase in a search bar that resembles Google. However, the Google logo is replaced by the word Blackle, and the white background has been changed to black.[2] The user enters the phrase "What is a black meme?" and a number of search results are displayed. This reference to digital media is makes the process visible, although the video piece shifts to an edited series of clips. This references the reflexivity of digital visuality as well, as the media is being used in the process of inquiring about itself. The video piece then cuts to a black and white film leader, which is a reference to the beginning of the proper work, indicating that the initial images of the search engine being used was a type of prelude. This section contains a montage of Black figures from 1980's and 1990's popular culture in the US. These figures include music performers such as Nina Symone, and Michael Jackson, talk show host Arsenio Hall, and athlete Magic Johnson. There are clips from music video clips from Beyonce, the trial of OJ Simpson, and police dashboard camera footage of traffic stops. The video essay ends with a return to the initial Blackle search results. One page shows the results for a search of the term "Black," and the last shows the results for the phrase "black meme."

One motif that is used repeatedly throughout *Black Meme* (2020) is a circular spinning rainbow, known colloquially as the "rainbow wheel of death." This is a symbol used on Apple computers which indicates that a program is taking longer than expected to run. This symbol is shown much larger than normal, taking the entirety of the screen. This is also a reflexive reference, which one can assume relates to the images of Black figures being portrayed in some state of tension or dysfunction. The self-reflexive rainbow wheel is similar to the Blackle search that begins the piece, in that both remind the viewer that these images are being presented through, and possibly distorted by digital media.

In a lecture given on the work, Russell provides a theoretical background for the video essay. In her talk, she points to the concept of blackfishing, which she describes as such: "When non-black, often white people, pretend to be black on social media, using a combination of makeup, prosthetics, and even surgery to amplify this performance" (Russell, 2020). Russell aligns blackfishing with digital blackface, which are two aspects of the same degrading, imperialist force. Furthermore, she argues that the concept of the Black meme is central to how contemporary digital media are transmitted. The Black meme, for Russell, predates the digital, in fact, finding its origin in the middle passage, where the simultaneous violent erasure of African culture and the appropriation of said culture set the stage for popular media in the United States. This can be seen in *Black Meme* (2020) in the clips from D.W. Griffith's Birth of a Nation (1915), where actors in blackface present enslaved Africans as both hapless buffoons and violent subhumans. Along with these film clips, Russell includes a still image from the 1919 film Lime Kiln Field Day, which is considered to be the oldest surviving American film to feature Black actors. The still shows a kiss between actors Bert Williams and Odessa Warren Gray, which Russell (2020) identifies as critical for its depiction of love between two individuals.

One section of *Black Meme* (2020) that relates specifically to the concept of the internet meme features a voiceover describing the fad known as "Trayvoning." This was an internet fad where individuals photograph themselves lying on the ground with a can of Arizona iced tea and a bag of Skittles, emulating the 2012 murder of Trayvon Martin. The unidentified voiceover implores white people to stop the practice. In a related section of her lecture, Russell identifies the role that lynching photographs played in initiating a viral media that predates the release of both films. In this manner, the lynching photograph are replaced by the digital images where predominantly white individuals lie face down on the ground, mocking the violent death of Martin at the hands of George Zimmerman, who was found not guilty of the murder.

Now that some basic elements of digital visuality have been used to analyze aspects of *How Can You Love Me and Hate Me at the Same Time?* (2011) and *Black Meme* (2020), I will turn to a broader discussion of contemporary social media and its relationship to digital visual art, in order to identify opportunities for them to be better understood, analyzed, and taught through a Digital Visual Art Education-based approach to making, teaching, and learning through digital visual art.

Social Media, Memes, and Digital Visual Art

Social media is a term that is very challenging to define. In the edited text The Social Media Reader, Mandiberg (2012) identifies this challenge through the various names that have been used to describe social media:

> Despite the widespread participant engagement and scholarly interest in this phenomenon, it has no definitive name. It has been given many names, a selection of the most prevalent of which include the corporate media favorite "user-generated content," Henry Jenkins's media-industries-focused "convergence culture," Jay Rosen's "the people formerly known as the audience," the politically infused "participatory media," Yochai Benkler's process-oriented "peer production," and Tim O'Reilly's computer-programming-oriented "Web 2.0." Each of these terms defines one separate aspect of the phenomenon and does so from the specific point of view of the different actors in this system (p. 2).

Mandiberg goes on to define each of these names, and to argue that the term social media speaks to each effectively: "'Social media' is a broad enough term that it can encompass, while preserving, each of these perspectives and their respective terms" (p. 4). It is beyond the scope of this text to analyze all aspects of social media.[3] Instead, I would like to focus here on the specific example of the meme, as it crosses numerous platforms and engages with digital media theory and methods in curious and illustrative ways.

As previously discussed, the concept of the meme was first developed by evolutionary biologist Richard Dawkins in 1972. Memes are therefore not a product of digital media. However, the ways that networked digital media help to appropriate and distribute information makes social media in particular the perfect environment for the meme:

> Conceptually born into this world as an eminently adaptable element, it has to be remembered that this entails not only being adaptable to new conditions, but adaptable by them: the Internet (with its ads and apps) has, transformationally and irrevocably, adapted the meme. (Bristow, 2019, pp. 16–17)

Shifman (2013) defines the meme as it relates to digital culture as such: "Three main attributes ascribed to memes are particularly relevant to the analysis of contemporary digital culture: (1) a gradual propagation from individuals to society, (2) reproduction via copying and imitation, and (3) diffusion through competition and selection" (p. 18). Wark and Wark

(2019), referencing Shifman, clarify how the internet meme differs from other viral media:

> The Internet meme is of a class of media that has emerged with distributed, platform-based networks. In Limor Shifman's simple and compelling definition, three qualities characterize it: it's collectively produced; it mutates; and it circulates. While it shares some qualities with like media—viral media also circulate; spam is collectively produced—it also differs from them. Memes are not only passed along, they are remade, varied, altered (p. 293).

In my elaboration of Digital Visual Art Education, it is relevant to ask the following: Is a meme is a work of digital art? I am going to bypass that question for the time being. Although it might be relevant, it would guide my analysis into areas that are unrelated, though they might be interesting. More relevant to my analysis is how memes operate within a digital visual culture. I will speak to the qualities identified above to explore this relationship. I will also explore how these qualities relate to digital visual works of art. These aspects will first be addressed as they relate to the concept of digital visuality.

It is important to first see how memes can be interpreted through the theory of digital visuality that I developed in Chapter One and applied to the work of Donnett earlier. In this theory, works of digital visual art are better understood through the concepts of interconnectedness and reflexivity, indeterminateness and variability, and intersectionality and power. Visibility in general refers to the process by which digital visual works are created and shared. Here, the process of making and sharing memes could not be any more visible. The meme form that has become dominant is the image appropriated from popular culture with block lettering, white with a black drop shadow, at the top and the bottom of the image. It is immediately recognizable and, more importantly, reproduceable. It is quite simple to use rudimentary programs such as MS Paint to combine text and image in meme fashion. If this is not an option there are numerous websites such as memegenerator.net and imgflip.com that allow users to make memes quickly and effortlessly. What is essential for most internet memes is that they do not represent an attempt to use digital imagery software in a proficient manner. This is what Douglas (2014) calls the Internet Ugly aesthetic.

The ability to make and share memes makes them a potent form of digital communication. Throughout this text, I have been using the model of the decentralized network that is drawn from electronic communication. As I mentioned in the introduction, I will clearly indicate the specific type of decentralization to which I refer. When discussing memes, it is most relevant to discuss them as a form of communication, as Shifman (2013) argues. Memes combine words and image to share a message, and in this manner they are related to any number of forms of communication that exist within a digital visual culture: advertisements, propaganda, infographics, and medical imaging all use similar components, but with very different goals. Memes tend to fall into the category of jokes (Yoon, 2016), but they are not always intentionally humorous. As Bristow (2019) writes:

> Memes present an indeterminate face; their messages, if in earnest, often verge so much on the absurd that it is difficult to tell if they're irony or iron-fistedness. Indeed, with many memes, satire is in the irony of the beholder. The range of responses in typical comments sections (encompassing earnestness, gullibility, failure to "get" the joke, trolling) is indicative here. Memes become, and are infinitely open to becoming, overdetermined (p. 129).

As indicated in this quote, memes are often hard to interpret, especially to the observer that is unfamiliar with their particular vernacular and presentational mode. Abreu (n.d.) proposes that the internet has helped to create a space where cultural appropriation is popularized and perpetuated. They call the online appropriation of Black culture digital blackface and uses the example of the #realni**ahours meme to illustrate this theory. This meme represents, for Abreu, the fringes of internet culture where racist forms of expression are reproduced, replicated, and normalized in the process. Here we have a model of multilevel communication in operation that is similar to the electronic networks theorized by Baran (1964).[4] In racist memes like #realni**ahours image and text combine to confuse and insult the viewer. The images are crude, pixelated copies of popular visual culture images borrowed from sources such as SpongeBob SquarePants and celebrities such as Brendan Frasier. The text is usually a version of asking who is still awake and asking them to "smash" the like button. These are opportunities for engagement and potential collaboration that are borrowed from previous memes and that are closely connected to the concept of interconnected reflexivity described in the previous chapter.

Social media are generally thought of as being more participatory than previous media forms. However, this general perception leads to some confusion between sharing and collaboration, as Hyde, et al (2012) describe: "User-generated content and social media create the tendency for confusion between sharing and collaboration. Sharing of content alone does not directly lead to collaboration" (p. 53) In terms of memes, the collaboration takes place in the sharing and appropriating, and is rarely made a part of the process. Memes are collaborative in the sense that individual meme creators respond to previous memes, and in the process create individual, isolated memes as well as an aggregate of memes:

> Social media platforms can become collaborative when they add an additional layer of coordination. On a microblogging platform like Twitter, this layer might take the form of an instruction to "use the #iranelections hashtag on your tweets," or on a photo-sharing platform, it might be an invitation to "post your photos to the LOLcats group." These mechanisms aggregate the content into a new social object. The new social object includes the metadata of each of its constituent objects; the author's name is the most important of this metadata. This creates two layers of content. Each shared individual unit is included in a cluster of shared units (pp. 53–54).

This relationship between the parts and the whole is directly related to the reflexivity that I have argued is an important element in digital visuality. In digital visuality, there is an interplay between what is seen and how it is seen. Here the reflexivity exists between the individual parts of the system—the nodes of the network, and the network itself. This is a self-similarity that is found in fractal formations that are an integral part of complex systems.[5] This is an apt comparison, as fractals are found in natural formations such as plant growth and cell development, while memes are based in genetic evolution. Christopher (2019) suggests that memes are only truly memes when they are being reproduced: "Memes only work if they move. If they are units of culture then in order to build and maintain that culture, they have to move" (p. 40). This leads to the concepts of indeterminateness and variability. I will discuss these concepts in more detail in Chapter Three but here I will outline their relevance as related to memes.

Memes display indeterminateness and variability as it relates to my concept of digital visuality offered in Chapter One. They are made of components that can easily be taken apart and recombined in any number of new ways, and in this fashion they are related to the concept of the remix (Shifman, 2013). In the example of #realni**ahours, the text has been replicated and altered slightly so that the reference to the original meme is maintained. This text is then added to a new image, and the process repeats itself, over and over again. This creates the movement that Christopher (2019) references, and it clearly demonstrates the connection between memes and genes. They cannot, however, stray too far from the prescribed meme format, lest they lose their particular force; more specifically, they lose the connection to those memes that have come before. As previously discussed, memes function as both the product of a single author and the product of the collective. This duality relates to collectivity, and it also unsettles previous concepts of authorial identity. As Donovan (2019) writes:

> Importantly, as memes are shared they shed the context of their creation, along with their authorship. Unmoored from the trappings of an author's reputation or intention, they become the collective property of the culture. As such, memes take on a life of their own, and no one has to answer for transgressive or hateful ideas. (n.p.)

Donovan writes of the power of memes to work as political weapons. She cites the use of memes by Russian hackers in the 2016 US Presidential election, which utilized existing social media platforms such as Twitter and Facebook to spread disinformation and divisiveness. In this manner Shifman's (2013) "diffusion through competition and selection" (p. 41) is provided with a genetic advantage: troll farms that amassed hundreds of workers were able to relentlessly interject memes into social media streams. These memes were focused on specific interest groups and were intended to further divide Americans. This is a form of power that is related to the dataveillance that was discussed in Chapter One, in that the memes are able to be tracked and monitored, giving the troll farms the ability to measure the effectiveness of their messaging through how often the images were shared, liked, or commented upon.

To summarize: The aspects of the internet meme that Shifman (2013) offered, and that Wark and Wark (2019) build upon, are directly related to the aspects of digital visuality that I theorized in Chapter One. Collectivity is related to the notion of visibility, where the means of production are clearly marked and easily accessed. This access makes the work more easily produced and distributed in a collective manner, which connects it to variability. Mutation also relates to the indeterminate variability of meme generation, where components are recombined in numerous ways, and with a variety of effects. Circulation relates to the interconnected reflexivity of digital visuality, as the process of replicating memes creates both individual memes while it impacts larger groups of memes that are related.[6]

Concepts of collectivity, mutation, and circulation can therefore help art, design, and media educators to better understand the ways that memes operate within a Digital Visual Art Education. It is this understanding that can influence approaches to teaching, researching, and making digital visual works of art. I will return to the digital visual work of art that I used to introduce this chapter, to explore the relevance of interconnectedness and reflexivity more fully. *How Can You Love Me and Hate Me at the Same Time?* (2011) by Nathaniel Donnett and *Black Meme* (2020) by Legacy Russell can be interpreted through the elements of digital visuality: particularly visibility and reflexivity. Here I will expand my readings of these pieces through the qualities of internet memes that I have addressed: collectivity, mutation, and circulation. My goal is to see how memes might help art educators to better research and therefore understand the ways that digital media relate to social media.

Visibility as part of a digital visuality relates to the modes of display that are enabled in the digital visual work of art. It is most closely related to the quality of collectivity that can be seen in internet memes. In Donnett's piece, the materials are simple, and can easily be seen in the displayed work. More importantly, the work is meant to be displayed. It takes the form of a protest sign that is intended to be held, to be used as a part of a protest, to be seen by others. There is a visibility that is inherent to the form the work takes. However, this form is undercut by the display if the work in a gallery setting. In this setting, the work is not held, and in the process the visibility is reduced. It is only through photographic reproduction that the work is seen by a wider audience. In *Black Meme* (2020), the piece is constructed from existing digital video clips and audio tracks. The way that these clips are composed make it clear that they are a montage, and the means of production are therefore easily accessed and achieved. The work is posted online, which provides an outlet for the work that extends beyond the traditional gallery or museum.

In terms of interconnected reflexivity, memes make reference to their means of production within a digital visual culture, and this relates to the concept of circulation. Individual memes circulate within a larger digital ecosystem, and they are altered through this process of feedback. This feedback loop speaks to the relationship between the individual and the society. In *How Can You Love Me and Hate Me at the Same Time?* (2011), the message that the work communicates is questioning general notions of subjectivity. The sign in the work states: "I AM A MEME." Earlier I asked: Who is "I?" Is it Nathaniel Donnett? Is it the viewer? Is it the sign itself? I will now speak to these questions, as I can better answer them having provided a basic outline for how memes function in digital visual culture. "I" would have to be variable in this statement, as it depends upon who is viewing the work. The protest signs from 1968 were held by Black men, and it was assumed that they were who the signs referred. In this work of digital visual art, no one is holding the sign. However, we should consider that the "I" is still referencing a Black subject, as the work makes reference to the sanitation strikes and to the artist. This connection to Black subjectivity is made clear in the title of *Black Meme* (2020). What is not clear is the identity of the user who is conducting the internet search.

How Can You Love Me and Hate Me at the Same Time? (2011) and *Black Meme* (2020) open up questions regarding the boundaries of subjectivity as well as the power of self-representation. The power to control how one is presented gives one the ability to self-monitor. This self-monitoring is another form of surveillance, a point to which Syms (2017) eludes when she states: "Representation is a sort of surveillance." (St. Felix, n.p.) Both works by Donnett and Russell speak to the complexities of Black representation through their works. These are forms of representation that are specific to the Black experience in the United States. However, they can also speak to experiences of other identity groups. The qualities of digital visuality that I have discussed with regards to these experiences are critical for an understanding of how digital visual works of art should be discussed, analyzed, and taught. In order to expand this conversation, I will now turn my discussion to another form of digital visuality that can help to further expand the concepts of interconnectedness and reflexivity: Data visualization

Data Visualization

Data visualization is a term that represents a diverse range of images. As stated by IBM Cloud Education: "Data visualization is the representation of data through use of common graphics, such as charts, plots, infographics, and even animations. These visual displays of information communicate complex data relationships and data-driven insights in a way that is easy to understand" (2021, n.p.). This description is telling, as the last sentence refers to complex data relationships being presented in a manner that is easily understood. This could easily refer to many of the digital visual works of art that I have discussed in previous chapters.

The main distinction that I would like to emphasize here is in the intent of the maker of the image. The use of the term communication here implies that there is a clear message contained in the data visualization. Furthermore, the data visualization is intended to provide a form of communication that clarifies any confusion that the vast and oftentimes messy data represents.

Digital visual artists, on the other hand, generally do not claim to provide any such clarity. The artists that I have discussed previously do not speak to the specific communicational aspects of their work. And when they do, it is not presented as an easy task. In fact, it could be argued that digital visual artists make the process of understanding large sets of data more complicated. The work of Hasan Elahi speaks directly to this complication, and the implications for data visualization as related to social interaction and personal liberty.

In order to further explore the relationship between data visualization and interconnected reflexivity, I will look at the work of Dennis Delgado. As it states on his personal website:

> Dennis Delgado was born in the South Bronx, and received a BA in Film Studies from the University of Rochester as well as an MFA in Sculpture from the City College of New York (CUNY). His work examines the forms through which ideologies of colonialism persist and re-inscribe themselves, revealing a historical presence in the current moment. He is interested in how technologies of vision reproduce the scopic regimes of expansionism and neo-liberal governance (Delgado, n.p.)

Delgado uses a variety of technologies and approaches in his work. In the series titled The Dark Database (2021), he presents images that are based on a traditional frontal photographic portrait. However, these images are synthesized from all images of faces from movies directed by directors of color. As Delgado states:

> The Dark Database series looks at the bias inherent in facial recognition systems. Using Open Computer Vision and the programming language Python, a facial detection algorithm was run on a series of films by directors of color. Each of the faces detected was stacked and centered according to a portrait template. The median pixel value for each detected face is calculated to create one single portrait of the film that serves as a kind of record of all the faces the facial detection algorithm was able to detect (n.p.).

The result is a single image for each film that combines all portraits that were detected, while leaving blank those that were harder to detect due to the implicit racial biases in the software. Delgado is making specific reference to these types of software in this series, and how they have been programmed to recognize those with lighter skin complexions.

> Current studies show that facial recognition systems are less able to detect a face in an image when the skin tone of that face is not Caucasian. The undetected faces are then not enrolled in the systems' database. As a result many of the systems are trained

> using datasets which contain fewer people of color, making those same systems inaccurate when recognizing or identifying individuals of color. The Dark Database is a kind of record of visibility and representation as seen through the eyes of artificial intelligence (n.p.).

When we compare The Dark Database to the description of data visualization presented earlier, we can see that the work does simplify the information presented in these films. Hundreds of thousands of individual frames are combined into one still image. However, the linear narrative of the film, which has become a familiar cultural text, is replaced by a static image that is not necessarily easier to understand.

The four aspects of digital visuality that might help artists, designers, educators, and researchers to work with and through digital visual art are interconnectedness, indeterminateness, interactivity, and intersectionality. Interconnectedness and the related concept of reflexivity describe the ways that contemporary digital media are networked in complicated ways that allow for the user to reflect upon various aspects of the experience, and of themselves, through the process. In The Dark Database (2021), we see a series of portraits that are in varying states of legibility. The portrait, as a Western artistic convention, is recognizable to many as a form of art that speak to identity and the self. As such, it is also a conveyor of racial stereotypes and white supremacy (Coates, 2009).

The Dark Database (2021) is not interconnected in the same manner as some of the previously discussed digital visual works. It does not exist within a dynamic state as in the case of *Tracking Transience* (2003–present), nor does it exist in multiple states as in *My Hands Wishful Thinking* (2001). It does, however, exist on the internet, which makes the work inherently unstable, and open to further revision. The reflexive nature of the portraits presented is similar to other portraits in the Western photographic tradition. In comparison to these portraits, The Dark Database (2021) allows for reflection on the history and function of the photographic portrait; how the images of those in power have been reproduced while those who have been marginalized are excluded from these processes.

There is, however, an interesting historical example that relates to this marginalization, and the use of data visualization by artists of color. At the end of the 19th century, the American sociologist W.E.B. DuBois helped to create 60 data visualizations for the Paris World's Fair which was held in 1900. These works, called infographics, were intended to communicate information about the progress of Black Americans. As Mansky (2018) writes:

> The way DuBois wielded this data to convey these realities was pioneering, but so, too, were the visual aesthetics of the infographics. Munro, who wrote the captions for each of the plates, came to see Du Bois as an innovator in design. In the book, he positions the data visualizations as "infographic activism" in their ability to get to the heart of inequities of the day. But he also points out that the compelling art, which was done in ink, gouache watercolor, graphite and photographic prints, deserves to be considered in its own right. The team's Modernist use of shape, color and structure, created just before the rise of Europe's avant-garde movements, he argues, makes the work nothing less than visionary (n.p.).

There have, of course, been a wide variety of artists of color who have used elements of data visualization in their work. Felix Gonzalez-Torres is one notable example. However, the contemporary field of data visualization seems to be dominated by white men. The reasons for this are manifold, and beyond the scope of this chapter. In keeping with the theme of intersectionality, discussed in detail in Chapter Four, the power imbalances in data visualization are features that should be further researched by those in art, design, and media studies. At this point I will look at data visualization through the concepts identified in the previous discussion of memes and digital virality: Collectivity, mutation, and circulation.

In terms of collectivity, data visualizations are often the products of work done by groups of people; designers and programmers collaborate on works that attempt to distill large amounts of data into simplified visual form. In the example of The Dark Database (2021), it is Delgado who is creating the work using the power of contemporary image processing software. However, his work relies upon the collectivity of the motion picture industry, which is composed of thousands of individuals who help to bring films to the viewer and the theatre or streaming platform. Collectivity is therefore an important element in how we understand data visualization in general, and specifically how power and race are addressed by Delgado in this work.

Mutation is the second element of digital virality that was discussed previously. As memes are created and distributed they mutate; the visual components are altered and the meaning changes as a result. There is not a direct corollary to be found in the ways that data visualization are created and shared. However, one might find a relevant connection in the ways that data visualizations build from one another, utilizing different data sets and morphing the structure in the process. In The Dark Database (2021), the work is not transmitted through digital channels in the ways that memes propagate and thrive. However, this work does speak to elements of mutation in the way that Delgado's software compiles and layers images from the films made by directors of color that he has selected. In this manner, the visible image is composed of numerous underlying images, each mutating as a new image is placed on top. The work is a record of the film as a whole, communicated through the faces (and races) of the actors that are present.

Circulation is the last attribute that is critical to an understanding of how memes operate within a digital visual culture. As cited earlier, Christopher (2019) refers to this process when he states: "Memes only work if they move. If they are units of culture then in order to build and maintain that culture, they have to move" (p. 40). Works of data visualization certainly circulate through networked digital communication channels in a manner similar to that of memes. The main difference here is that circulation for the meme is essential for the meme to function. Circulation does not play a similar role in the functioning of data visualizations. On a general level, they gain more viewership the more that they are circulated, but this circulation does not play a role in how they are viewed or interpreted.

In order to further explore the relationship between interconnected reflexivity and digital visual art in the forms of memes and data visualizations, I will look to the concept of hypertext, as it informs both data visualization in digital visual art and can lead into a discussion of educational approaches that are derived from such processes and concepts.

Hypertext and Data Visualization

Hypertext is a concept that has its roots in postwar American information science. As Landow (1989) writes:

> Writers on hypertext trace the notion to a pioneering article by Vannevar Bush in the 1945 Atlantic Monthly that called for mechanically linked information-retrieval machines to help scholars and decision-makers in the midst of what was already becoming an explosion of information (Bush, 1945). In the 1960s Douglas C. Englebart and Theodor H. Nelson began to design and implement computer systems that could implement some of these notions of linked texts, and today hypertext as a term refers almost exclusively to electronic hypertext systems that rely on computing equipment and software (p. 174).

Innumerable aspects of contemporary life have been affected by the linkages that are represented in the term hypertext. Art educators have written about the integration of hypertext-based digital technologies in art classrooms

(Kiefer-Boyd, 1996; Tavin, 2002; Taylor & Carpenter, 2002), and some have started to explore the potential for lattice-like curricular structures that resemble simplified network structures (May, 2011). While hypertext represented a model for addressing the influence of digital media on art educational systems, and promised to reform outdated pedagogical approaches, it nonetheless remained rooted to hierarchical and patriarchal ideological forces (Payne, 2018).

Data visualizations generally are intended to simplify the complex sets of connections that make up hypertextual systems. I am both intrigued and skeptical of the use of data visualization as a research tool in academia. Both of these responses are heightened in the specific case of art educational data visualization, primarily due to the visual nature of the content of our field, and the visual qualities of data visualization. It is important to look at the relationship between data visualization and hypertext for the following reasons. First, they both seek to makes sense of large sets of data. Hypertext comes from the fields of cybernetics and computer science, while data visualization is a hybrid category that is informed equally by graphic design, visual art, and information science. Second, the connections between the two forms of visuality might help to provide art, design, and media scholars with useful information about their potential application in educational settings. And last, an analysis of this relationship might provide useful information for the further development of a Digital Visual Art Education.

One final relevant form of interconnectedness that I will discuss here is the way that data visualization in the form of hypertext is presented in popular visual culture. One of the most prominent examples are the networks of image and text that are used in crime dramas and thrillers. These hypertextual networks are called evidence walls.[7] Evidence wall is the catch-all term for the boards on which investigators, or sometimes criminals, pin up and plot out all their clues in crime and spy thrillers, and recently it has become unthinkable for almost any serious TV drama not to have some sort of board for the characters to contemplate as they try to work out the kinks of a theory (Benson, 2015). Evidence walls in popular visual culture are often crafted out of photos and string in through relatively low-tech means. Other forms of evidence walls use a variety of high-tech devices and means and approach the limits of what is currently available to the average consumer. The crime fighting software used to predict violations in Minority Report is an excellent example of this approach.

Benson (2015) cites numerous examples of evidence walls from recent popular media, including: Wire, True Detective, Serial, Before I Go to Sleep, A Most Wanted Man, Amazing Spider Man 2, Fargo, Sherlock, The Bridge. The history of the evidence wall started with Cold War spy thrillers such as Tinker Tailor Soldier Spy. The first popular use of an evidence wall in popular media can be seen in Dr. Strangelove (1964). It has increasingly figured as a plot point in a wide variety of thrillers and dramas. There are a number of variants of the evidence wall that are inevitably connected with the unstable mental state of the creator.

Designer Rob Treen describes the relationship between data visualization in the form of the evidence wall and education as such:

> You have to remember, we've grown up in a culture where people use mind maps, spider diagrams, flow charts and other visualisations of information all the time in education and at work. It means that a lot of people are geared to seeing a wall as a way of showing what a character is thinking. They are visual shorthand, which is important when screen time is at a premium—sometimes in the edits you're shaving half-seconds off scenes. And modern viewers don't want be slapped in the face with something that is obviously there to move the plot along. You know, someone saying, 'Oh, you've drawn a picture of the devil, so you must be evil'. With a wall you can show clues and let the viewer understand it (Benson, 2015, n.p.).

This is a useful comment for the Digital Visual Art Education as it relates to art, design, and media education. As Treen posits, our educational forms of data visualization are influencing how data is visualized in our popular visual culture. This is a point that should be taken up by art educators, design educators, and media educators. If these educators were to integrate data visualization approaches that are critical of marginalization and oversimplification, would the popular media change as a result? If educators were to engage with the messy and multifaceted aspects of meme production—collectivity, mutation, and circulation—could opportunities for critical reflection and socially aware making be made more accessible? I will speak to these questions in the conclusion to this book. In the next chapter, I will turn to the concept of indeterminate variability as it relates to a Digital Visual Art Education.

Notes

1 Brown (2016) places this piece within the historical lineage of the visual culture of the Civil Rights movement.

2 Blackle is an energy saving search engine developed by Google, which saves energy by using back instead of white. These savings are contested, however.

3 In the previous chapter, I analyzed YouTube as it relates to digital visual works of art, and I will draw upon this chapter where relevant to social media in general, and memes specifically.

4 Baran theorized that communications networks in the future would have to accommodate different types of communications, from microwave signals to TV broadcasts to telephone cable links to satellite links (p. 5).

5 In Dysfunction and Decentralization in New Media Art and Education (2015). I discuss how the fractal is taken up by curriculum theorists as seen in Davis, B., Sumara, D., and Luce-Kapler, R. (2000), for example. I compare and contrast the model of the fractal with decentralized networks specifically in Chapter Three.

6 In addition the intersectional power of circulation through social media also involves the ability to monitor and track memes in a manner that is central to contemporary methods of dataveillance. This concept will be discussed in detail in Chapter Four.

7 Evidence walls are colloquially known as "crazy walls." This is a term that is ableist, and so I will use the term "evidence wall" in this chapter.

References

Abreu, M. A. (n.d.). Online Imagined Black English. In D. Howard, (Ed.), *Arachne #0—on Gender, Labour and Technology*. Retrieved from https://arachne.cc/issues/01/index.html

Baran, P. (1964). On Distributed Communications Networks. *IEEE Transactions of the Professional Technical Group on Communication Systems, CS-12*(1). RAND Corporation.

Benson, R. (2015). Decoding the Detective's 'Crazy Wall.' *Esquire*. https://www.esquire.com/uk/culture/film/news/a7703/detective-show-crazy-walls/

Bristow, D. (2019a). Introproduction. In D. Bristow & A. Bown (Eds.), *Post Memes: Seizing the Memes of Production* (pp. 17–24). Punctum Books. https://doi.org/10.2307/j.ctv11hptdx.3

Bristow, D. (2019b). The Work of Art(iculation) in the Age of Memic Rhythmicality: Memes between Form, Content, and Structure. In D. Bristow & A. Bown (Eds.), *Post Memes: Seizing the Memes of Production* (pp. 115–136). Punctum Books.

Christopher, R. (2019). The Meme Is Dead, Long Live the Meme. In A. Bown & D. Bristow (Eds.), *Post Memes: Seizing the Memes of Production* (pp. 31–44). Punctum Books.

Coates, T. (2009). Portraiture, Colonialism and Racism. *The Atlantic*. Accessed June 22, from https://www.theatlantic.com/entertainment/archive/2009/07/portraiture-colonialism-and-racism/22513/

Dawkins, R. (1976). *The Selfish Gene*. Oxford.

Delgado, D. (n.d.). *Dennis Delgado*. Retrieved March, 2023, from: https://www.delgadostudio.net

Donnett, N. (2011). *How Can You Love Me and Hate Me at the Same Time? (Artwork)*.

Donovan, J. (2019). How Memes Got Weaponized: A Short History. *MIT Technology Review*. Accessed from https://www.technologyreview.com/2019/10/24/132228/political-war-memes-disinformation/

Douglas, N. (2014). It's Supposed to Look Like Shit: The Internet Ugly Aesthetic. *The Journal of Visual Culture*, *13*(3), 314–339.

DuBois, W. E. B. (1903). *The Souls of Black Folks*. A.C. McClurg & Co.

Elahi, H. (2003–present). *Tracking Transience* (artwork).

Fazal, M. (2018). Talking to the Guy Who Invented the Word Meme. And then It Got Weird. *Vice Magazine*. Accessed February, 2023, from https://www.vice.com/en/article/d35ana/talking-to-the-guy-who-invented-the-word-meme-richard-dawkins

Hyde, A., Linksvayer, M., Kanarinka, Mandiberg, M., Peirano, M., Tarka, S., & Zer-Aviv, M. (2012). What Is Collaboration Anyway? In Mandiberg M. (Ed.), *The Social Media Reader* (pp. 53–68). NYU Press. Retrieved March, 2023, from http://www.jstor.org/stable/j.ctt16gzq5m.9

IBM Cloud Education. (2021). *What Is Data Visualization*. Retrieved February, 2023, from https://www.ibm.com/topics/data-visualization

Jackson, Z. (2013). Animal: New Directions in the Theorization of Race and Posthumanism. *Feminist Studies*, 39(3), 669–685. Retrieved March, 2023, from http://www.jstor.org/stable/23719431

Kiefer-Boyd, K. (1996). Interfacing Hypermedia and the Internet with Critical Inquiry in the Arts: Preservice Training. *The Journal of the National art Education Association* (54), 33–41.

Landow, G. P. (1989). Hypertext in Literary Education, Criticism, and Scholarship. *Computers and the Humanities*, *23*(3), 173–198. http://www.jstor.org/stable/30200162

Mandiberg, M. (2012). Introduction. In M. Mandiberg (Ed.), *The Social Media Reader* (pp. 1–10). NYU Press. Accessed from http://www.jstor.org/stable/j.ctt16gzq5m.4

Mansky, J. (2018). W.E.B. Du Bois' Visionary Infographics Come Together for the First Time in Full Color. *Smithsonian Magazine*. Retrieved March, 2023, from https://www.smithsonianmag.com/history/first-time-together-and-color-book-displays-web-du-bois-visionary-infographics-180970826/

May, H. (2011). Shifting the Curriculum: Decentralization in the Art Education Experience. *Art Education*, 64(3), 33–40. Retrieved March, 2023, from http://www.jstor.org/stable/23034053

Obadike, K., & Obadike, M. (2001). *My Hands Wishful Thinking* (artwork).

Payne, R. (2018). *The Promiscuity of Network Culture: Queer Theory and Digital Media*. Routledge.

Russell, L. (n.d.). *Meet Legacy* (Webpage). Retrieved March, 2023, from https://www.legacyrussell.com/MEET-LEGACY

Russell, L. (2020). *Black Meme* (artwork).

Schifman, L. (2013). *Memes in Digital Culture*. MIT Press.

St. Felix, D. (2017). How to be a Successful Black Woman. *The New Yorker*. Accessed from https://www.newyorker.com/culture/persons-of-interest/how-to-be-a-successful-black-woman

Syms, M. (2015). Stages of Laughter 3. *ARTNews*. Retrieved March, 2023, from https://www.artnews.com/art-in-america/features/stages-of-laughter-3-martine-syms-63089/

Tavin, K. (2002). Engaging Advertisements: Looking for Meaning in and through Art Education. *Visual Arts Research*, 28(2), 38–47.

Taylor, P., & Carpenter, S. (2002). Inventively Linking: Teaching and Learning with Computer Hypertext. *The Journal of the National Art Education Association*, 55(4), 6–12.

Wark, S., & Wark, M. (2019). Circulation and Its Discontents. In A. Bown & D. Bristow (Eds.), *Post Memes: Seizing the Memes of Production* (pp. 293–318). Punctum Books.

Yoon, I. (2016). Why Is It Not Just a Joke? Analysis of Internet Memes Associated with Racism and Hidden Ideology of Colorblindness. *Journal of Cultural Research in Art Education*, 33, 92–123.

· 3 ·

INDETERMINATE: DIGITAL VISUAL MAKING AND POST-DIGITAL MATERIALITY

In this chapter I will turn my attention to the relationship between digital visual art and the concept of indeterminacy and the related concept of variability. Specifically, I will look at work that challenges notions of materiality and ways of making that have become central to art, media, and design education through the majority of the 20th century. The concept of the post-digital will help to speak to these challenges. Specifically, digital works made using Artificial Intelligence (AI) and Non-fungible Token (NFT) art both disrupt aspects of authorship that many digital artworks have, perhaps paradoxically, emphasized. In addition to AI works of digital art I will discuss the relationship between digital art and the ways of making that are currently being seen in makerspaces. In order to determine the value of the post-digital making as it relates to a Digital Visual Art Education, I will first look at the work of digital visual artist Simone Giertz. In a field that is made of hobbyists, crafters, and amateur engineers making very useful things her work stands out, primarily because of its uselessness.

In the TED talk titled "Why You Should Make Useless Things" (2018), Giertz discusses the importance of solving problems in indirect, absurd, and comical ways. She chooses to complete everyday tasks like brushing your teeth through the creation of what she calls "useless machines." She taught herself to make these machines through a process that she describes as such:

> I got interested in making robots, and I wanted to teach myself about hardware. But building things with hardware, especially if you are teaching yourself, is something that's really difficult to do. It has a high likelihood of failure, it has a high likelihood of making you feel stupid. And that was my biggest fear at the time.

Giertz chose to use her developing engineering skills to make machines that were intended to fail. She describes this process as actually being quite smart, because as the machine failed, it removed the fear of failure. The performance anxiety that Giertz personally struggled with was replaced by a sense of enthusiasm and play.

The enthusiasm that Giertz felt for these useless machines soon faded, however. After developing a large YouTube following for her wacky devices, she decided to apply her engineering skills to projects that would actually work. The most popular of these decidedly useful machines is a vehicle that she calls Truckla. Truckla is a Tesla automobile that Giertz modified so that it has a truck bed in the rear of the vehicle. She has stated that her shift to more serious projects is in some ways a response to the useless machines, and the way that her approach to building them placed her in a position where she was self-deprecating to the point where she was not taken seriously (Goode, 2019).

Each of these works by Giertz raises questions about the relationship between making and digital technologies and are relevant examples of the contemporary intersection of creative expression and digital technology, of low-tech Arduino circuits and household objects mixed with high-tech automobile engineering and digital filmmaking. They also relate to the concepts of indeterminacy and variability that I am proposing are important elements in digital visuality, and therefore a Digital Visual Art Education.

Indeterminacy and variability are qualities shared by many digital works of art. Digital works of art tend to be indeterminate both in their structure and their function. The use of digital media, and coding languages specifically, allow for digital works to be disassembled and reassembled with ease. As these works are remixed and rethought, the finished work of art is made variable. This variability draws into question notions of media specificity and stability that are central to many artistic traditions. Post-digital art speaks directly to this variability, as the nature of digitality is brought into question. The work of Jennifer Chan stands as an excellent example of post-digital art, raising questions that are specific to this conversation: What does it mean for a work of art to be digital when innumerable aspects of daily life are interconnected in and through digital media?

In order to more fully explore the relationship between indeterminacy, variability, and post-digital materiality, I will discuss the cultural influences that have make the work of Giertz so compelling. These influences can be seen in what is called the maker movement. The maker movement developed primarily through DIY technology initiatives that had taken many forms: hackerspaces, computing clubs, and hobbyist gatherings, to name a few. The most influential of these were gatherings known as Maker Faires. Maker Faires were created by Dale Dougherty, founder and executive chairman of Maker Media, and Sherry Huss, vice president of Maker Media (http://makerfaire.com/makerfairehistory/). These gatherings have, since 2006, allowed both amateur and professional tech hobbyists to gather and share techniques, and to sell their products to the public (Bajarin, 2014). They were initially an outgrowth of Make Magazine, which is published by Maker Media. Maker Media has been instrumental in bringing makerspaces into US public high schools, primarily through a grant from the Defense Advanced Research Projects Agency (DARPA). This funding source is quite controversial due to the connection between public education and military research (Dougherty, 2012).

The maker movement has been taken up by those advocating for science, technology, engineering, and math (STEM) educational approaches. Emphasis on STEM Education in United States Public Schools was linked with US President Barack Obama's Race to the Top District Program, which provided Department of Education funds for approaches to learning that were considered individualized and rigorous (http://www.ed.gov/stem). Corporations, educational advocacy groups, and the US Government have partnered to advance STEM initiatives in public school, after-school programs, and community spaces. The 2015 reauthorization of the Elementary and Secondary Education Act guaranteed over $150,000,000 in funding for STEM education (Brown, 2015), further reinforcing the governmental support of STEM fields.

STEM education and Maker Faires both represent compelling reference points for a Digital Visual Art Education, for the following reasons. First, STEM education emphasizes individualized learning that is student-centered and experiential. As promoted by the US Department of Education, STEM education represents a bureaucratic, top-down approach to learning. Maker Faires, on the other hand, extend beyond the confines of pre-K-12 education, to address learning in a variety of spaces and at a variety of ages conceptualized as grassroots, community-based collaborative events. The meeting of the two in the form of the educational makerspace has great potential for fusing the best of both worlds. However, the makerspace in educational practice also has the potential to sap the spontaneous, rhizomatic qualities that many find a compelling component of the maker movement.

Art, design, and media educators who are invested in these intersections can learn from this example, as it entails notions of creativity, consumerism, and social class. Giertz represents a contemporary nexus of histories of free play and creative self-expression, Do-It-Yourself (DIY) strategies, and technological exploration. Those interested in a Digital Visual Art Education-based approach to making, learning, and teaching digital visual art should explore how the histories of artistic exploration and creative self-expression drawn from art, design, and media education relate to the DIY applications of digital media related to the maker movement, to attempt to determine what one might learn from the other.

Much of the history of art education, for example, is rooted in standardized forms of making represented by the industrial drawing movement, through the creative self-expression era where individual expression was paramount. These approaches have led into our current milieu that abounds with phrases such as 21st Century Skills and Choice-Based Artmaking. While the media and methods have changed with the times, making art continues to be central to art education. In the late 20th Century, this emphasis upon making was questioned by those advocating for the incorporation of visual culture-based art educational approaches. (See Freedman, 2003).

However, the emphasis on production was questioned well before the turn of the 21st century. During the early 20th century John Dewey (1916) promoted a vision of art education that in many ways prefigured the maker movement. Dewey was an outspoken progressive educator who questioned the reliance upon outmoded educational approaches in texts such as Democracy and Education (1916), while he also speaks to the challenges inherent in artmaking and viewing. In his later book Art as Experience (1937), he writes:

> Refusal to acknowledge the boundaries set by convention is the source of frequent denunciations of objects of art as immoral. But one of the functions of art is precisely to sap the moralistic timidity that causes the mind to shy away from some materials and refuses to admit them into clear and purifying light of perceptive consciousness. (pp. 196–7)

This unconventional attitude towards the artistic experience is similar to the guiding philosophies of the maker movement. The primary focus of the maker movement has been to place emphasis upon the creative problem solving that can take place when learners interact with a wide variety of materials. However, a more direct philosophical influence that guides the maker movement can be found in Seymour Papert, an MIT professor who developed the concept of Constructionism (Halverson & Sheridan, 2014). Constructionism is an educational philosophy that looks at how the learner constructs knowledge for herself or himself (Papert & Harel, 1991). One can see Constructionism on full display in the work of Simone Giertz, particularly because she taught herself to code and construct her useless machines, which she also calls her "shitty robots." She created these primarily for her own entertainment. Just as many are excited by the work of Giertz, many educators are eager to see the ideas contained within Constructionism put into play in educational settings (Peppler, 2010).

Art, design, and media educators who wish to incorporate makerspace methods and post-digital ways of making should be sure to foreground making methods and theories, both historical and contemporary, that might ensure that the distinct elements of these educational approaches are not diminished. In addition to the critical modes of interpretation and art historical analysis mentioned earlier, it is also important for art educators to draw upon artists and art processes both contemporary and canonical. As such, I offer a few examples of artists who have informed my own makerspace-based activities in art educational spaces (Sweeny, 2017).

Rube Goldberg is an excellent historical example for the fields of art, design, and media education. He was a cartoonist who drew magnificently complicated machines. Although he did earn a degree in engineering, he was best known as an artist who used traditional means to make his art (Marzio, 1972). He became famous for his creative, clever contraptions, which typically demonstrated how one could complete a simple task through an unnecessarily complicated process. In this manner, his work is certainly relevant to the work made by Giertz. And just like Giertz, Goldberg also presented technology as a concept that could be satirized. This is an important lesson for those who might take our digital technologies perhaps too seriously.

Echo Yang is a contemporary artist who repurposes common household machines such as alarm clocks and Sony Walkman devices to make drawing machines, that then create drawings. She describes the process as one that reveals the internal algorithm of the machine (Zhang, 2014). Zhang's drawing machines show the extent to which artists can use technologies to make art without a complete understanding of the mechanical and electrical principles that make up the devices. This approach to common technologies is also similar to the way that Simone Giertz works, although her later work is decidedly more polished, as previously discussed.

Another excellent reference point for art, design, and media educators interested in the relationship between makerspaces and a Digital Visual Art Education is the E.A.T. (Engineering, Art, and Technology) group, who pioneered many explorations in these fields in the early 1960's. In fact, E.A.T. paired artists with engineers in order to see what both fields might learn from the other (Klüver, 1969). Pairing students with partners who are familiar with ways of making that are distinct from the visual arts in this manner may help them to see different way of working. Group projects between math, science, engineering, and art education students might lead to phenomenal results, if the process is open and the product is not narrowly defined.

None of these artists created works that use some of the more high-tech devices that are common to makerspaces, or in many of the useless machines created by Giertz. Perhaps this reflects my own familiarity, or lack thereof, with advanced digital technologies and coding languages. It also surely derives from my experiences as a public-school art educator in the US, where materials and budgetary support was generally limited. My intent in discussing their work is to show how a wide range of materials can be used and even misused, and in the process become demystified. This process of demystification is central to the notion of post-digital materiality.

Post-digital Materiality

The post-digital draws together notions of past and present in compelling and often confusing ways. The initial explorations of post-digital sound were intended to disrupt narratives of audio perfection and clarity that were part of digital music discussions in the late 20th century (Cramer, 2014). At the turn of the 21st century glitch-based works by Cascone (2000) took digital tools meant to present the listener with a friction-free listening experience and integrated sounds and techniques that related to previous audio media forms such as vinyl records. These glitch pieces pointed towards approaches to making music that could simultaneously look to the past and the future, and in this hybrid approach the post-digital is located.

Post-digital works of art employ a similar form of temporal simultaneity. *Ally (Nice White Person)* (2018) by Jennifer Chan makes a number of references to digital technologies and processes, while at the same time combining pop culture themes that are both contemporary and nostalgic. The plush figure of the Moomin character that wears these references is, in an important way, a stand in for the viewer, or perhaps even the artist herself. It is in this play with subjectivity and materiality that this work relates to the contemporary area of study known as Feminist New Materialism.

Feminist New Materialism is an interdisciplinary area of study that emerged at the beginning of the 21st century. It looks to denaturalize traditional concepts of agency and power that are rooted in Western epistemologies and ontologies (Sendcindiver, 2017). In the visual arts, new materialism has been instrumental in unsettling humanist concepts that differentiate between the object and the subject. These posthumanist theories have been most prominently argued in the sciences by Karen Barad (2007). They have also been applied to the visual arts by theorists such as Kate Mondloch (2018). Barad emphasizes the ways that Western, Cartesian concepts of materiality have failed to acknowledge the indeterminate nature of matter as shown through advanced scientific imaging technologies, while Mondloch builds a theory of materialism that is inherently feminist as it acknowledges the power that is coupled with material form.

The indeterminate nature of digital visual works of art should be read through Feminist New Materialism as a result of these qualities. However, my previous discussion of race and subjectivity from Chapter Two raises issues that critics of New Materialism have identified. As Thompkins (2016) states:

> There are reasons to be suspicious of the New Materialism, as indeed there are reasons to be suspicious of any intellectual movement that calls itself "new"—because of course we need to always ask: what is the heroic narrative that its putative "newness" seeks to instantiate? A non-human centered ontology and ethics; a sense of the biological and non-biological world as vital and alive; an idea of the body as having a life and conversation of its own, with itself; and, most centrally and crucially, the idea that planetary life should, must be, and will be at the determinative center of political world-making: these are epistemologies and ontologies that can hardly be said to have recently been invented but rather are familiar to, among others, First Nations and Indigenous peoples; to those humans who have never been quite human enough as explored, for instance, in postcolonial and revolutionary black thought; to some strands of feminist thinking, for instance, de Beauvoir's thinking about the objecthood of women; and to other non-Western medical and spiritual modalities.

This critique of new materialism points to a colonization of thought that we should take time to consider as we discuss the indeterminate nature of digital visual works of art as related to digital and post-digital making. In *Ally (Nice White Person)* (2018), we can consider the agency of the Moomin figure, and how it might function as a stand in for ourselves. We can also, by the same token, consider the subjectivity of the stool upon which the Moomin sits, or even the gallery space that surrounds the piece. In the "shitty robots" by Giertz, many mundane activities such as hair brushing are replaced by the actions of the robot. These actions are intentionally dysfunctional as they highlight the limits of machinic ability. The robots have a level of agency, but this proves to be fraught, as the actions inevitably fail. Failure is also a major element within the drawings of Goldberg, the drawing machines of Yang, and many of the projects organized by E.A.T. A Feminist New Materialist lens would help to reframe the ways that the individual interacts with the various technologies in each, challenging the agency of the human participant and acknowledging the role that the machines play in each.

All of these are relevant elements of a Feminist New Materialist perspective. These lines of thinking should be tempered by the issues raised by Thompkins (2016), who asks us to consider the ways that New Materialism, in general, is in fact not new. Along with the groups mentioned in the previous quote, one could also add the subjective positions represented by young people, for example. They would likely engage with figures such as the Moomin with little regard for the materiality or agency of the plush figure.

The subjectivity of the sign featured in *How Can You Love Me and Hate Me at the Same Time?* (2011) in Chapter Two, and the racial traits of memes, would also be a relevant topic for inquiry in a Feminist New Materialist-based Digital Visual Art Education. Here we have a reflexivity that is not universal. The "I" of the sign is not applicable to all who hold it, and memes, as Russell (2020) contends, are indeed Black if we consider the history of racial oppression and media distribution in the United States. In terms of variability, the elements that compose these works are quite different. However, one can consider that all works of art that are reproduced through digital means enter themselves into a space where they can be copied, cut, pasted, and reconceived. This is indeed a post-digital as well as a post-internet condition. *How Can You Love Me and Hate Me at the Same Time?* (2011) and *Ally (Nice White Person)* (2018) as well as the works by Giertz discussed previously are post-digital works not only because they refer to digital cultures, but also because they speak to these cultures through a variety of materialities and methods: some digital, some not.

All of these works have been constructed in a manner that shows how they were made. Giertz makes detailed videos that show her process, which is an integral component of art made and shown on YouTube. The process of making shown in *Ally (Nice White Person)* (2018) is a bit less obvious. However, there are indications that Chan is, at least, not trying to obscure the way that the piece has come together. The product tags on the Moomin figure are clearly visible, and the stool upon which the figure sits is easily recognizable as an object easily purchased at Ikea. In *How Can You Love Me and Hate Me at the Same Time?* (2011), Bennett's sign is relatively crude; the letters are frayed, which could be a reference to the time that has passed since the 1968 sanitation strike. It could also reference the wear and tear that accompanies the fight for racial justice in the United States.

The material qualities of digital visual works should be read through the notion of the poor image proposed by Stereyl (2009). The poor image speaks to the processes of appropriation and replication that are fundamental to digital communication. I previously used the notion of the poor image to talk about identity in digital visual works of art. Here, I would like to use the concept to talk about formal and material qualities of digital visual works of art. The work of Giertz, Chan, and Bennett are each intentionally worn. They bear signs of being used and they are certainly not fine art objects that are to be appreciated at a distance. The poor image, for Stereyl, is also a digital product that has been used. In this process it is distorted, pixilated, and degraded. The "shitty robots" that Giertz makes are a product of her process, which is self-initiated and led, as previously discussed. With regards to the materials that he uses, Donnett (2014) states:

> Formally I work in mixed media drawings paintings, installation, sculpture, and performance using everyday materials, objects, and participatory actions, along with African American cultural frameworks as conceptual and optical devices to comment on the contemporary human condition, everyday experience, art history, and contemporary art. (n.p.)

One can see that the reference the 1968 I AM A MAN protest signs relates to this use of African American cultural frameworks as conceptual and optical devices. Donnett also refers to these frameworks in his writings, which are posted on his website. In his writing titled Black Privilege (2020), Donnett presents a list of 35 ironic aspects of daily life that are favorable to those who identify as Black. Number ten is particularly relevant: "Black privilege is being able to be as late as you want to since your mental clock time is expected to be in a different zone. It is called CPT time" (n.p.) In this statement, Donnett is referring to "Colored Peoples Time." This is a racist concept that accuses Black people of being habitually late (Bates, 2016). This phrase is connected to the #realni**ahours meme discussed in the previous chapter. In this more explicit version, however, the difference in the perception of time is framed sarcastically as a positive trait. Russell (2020) also makes a connection between time and race in her Black Meme (2020) lecture. She references the essay titled Refusing Blackness-as-victimization: Trayvon Martin and the Black Cyborgs, written by Joao Costa Vargas and Joy A. James (2012). In this essay, Vargas and James make the following point: "Like all black children, Trayvon lived on borrowed, impossible time. The time is borrowed because as soon as the presumed innocence is over, their time as a sin-free, threat-free person ends" (p. 197).

In these works, the material qualities are overlayed with concepts of race, time, monetary value, and artistic craft. Each work speaks to the concept of materiality through a post-digital frame of reference. As qualities of a Digital Visual Art Education, indeterminacy and variability can allow artist, designers, and educators to look at the structural and functional aspects of the digital visual work of art. In *The Dark Database* (2021), by Dennis Delgado, we see a series of images where the features of the subjects are not clearly defined. The fuzziness of the images could be called indeterminate. However, this is not the way that I have been using the term in this book. Indeterminacy relates to the structure of many digital visual works of art that are able to be manipulated by the viewer, or through additional processes enabled by software or hardware. In this sense, *The Dark Database* (2021) is less indeterminate than many of the digital visual works of art that have been discussed previously.

As digital works, the images can still be seen on a variety of devices and manipulated through any number of programs and apps. The viewer can easily import one of the images into Photoshop, for example, and change the contrast so that the image is less dark. They can use a tool that can unblur an image, which would dramatically change its impact. This series of images also speaks to variability as it relates to contemporary digital surveillance technologies. The racial bias embedded in facial recognition software builds variability into a process that is intended to be clear and unbiased. In this manner, the fixed nature of the digital images in *The Dark Database* (2021) respond to the process by which individual software programmers and computer operators exert influence over automated processes.

Issues regarding the automation of digital artmaking can perhaps best be identified in the artistic production that employs AI. AI-based works of digital art harness the capabilities of large-scale computing networks and databases in order to allow the generation of images from text prompts:

> A.I. text-to-image generators such as Stable Diffusion, Midjourney and DALL-E … have become widely used to create all sorts of images, ranging from digital art pieces to character designs. Stable Diffusion alone has more than 10 million daily users. These A.I. products are built on collections of images known as "data sets," from which a detailed map of the data set's contents, the "model," is formed by finding the connections among images and between images and words. Images and text are linked in the data set, so the model learns how to associate words with images. It can then make a new image based on the words you type in (Anderson, 2022).

Artists who create data visualizations often use AI-based programs that allow them to make use of vast amounts of information. As Dennis Delgado (n.d.) states:

> Current studies show that facial recognition systems are less able to detect a face in an image when the skin tone of that face is not Caucasian. The undetected faces are then not enrolled in the systems' database. As a result many of the systems are trained using datasets which contain fewer people of color, making those same systems inaccurate when recognizing or identifying individuals of color. The Dark Database is a kind of record of visibility and representation as seen through the eyes of artificial intelligence (n.p.).

Delgado identifies the racist underpinnings of facial recognition software and uses these programs to reflect these inherent biases back to the viewer through his AI-generated data visualizations. AI is poised to have an impact on numerous fields in the visual arts. Some of these fields already use advanced digital technologies, such as CGI in the motion picture industry, while others rely upon more traditional media, such as hand rendered comics.

The artist Sarah Anderson has described the impact that AI-generated images had on her web-based comics as well as her artistic identity, in the opinion piece titled The Alt-Right Manipulated My Comic. Then A.I. Claimed It (2022). In this piece, Anderson describes the process by which her webcomic was initially appropriated by individuals from the alt-right. These appropriations used comic images that she had created and paired them with text that aligned with alt-right ideologies such as Holocaust denial and general

Neo-Nazism. She describes this as a violation of not only her artistic rights, but her personal beliefs and political affiliations. Then, she goes on to detail the ways that AI text-to-image generators were able to appropriate her comics, reproducing them in style but not content. This, she fears, is a violation that is far worse than the appropriations by the far right. AI generators such as Stable Diffusion are based on data sets that are accessible by the public. These data sets include a great deal of pornographic and violent content, so the intentional appropriations of her work by the alt-right could, with the click of a mouse button, be multiplied and magnified to almost limitless degrees.

The ethical implications of such practices add important nuance to the discussion of indeterminacy and variability as they relate to a Digital Visual Art Education. Digital works of art tend to be indeterminate both in their structure and their function while the materiality of digital works allow for digital works to be made variable. These processes should not be seen as neutral. Indeterminacy opens up the potential for digital works of art to be manipulated in ways that might be far from what the artist intended. This manipulation might be benign, but as we have seen in the example of Sarah Anderson, it can also result in works that are offensive and hateful.

AI-based artmaking will only continue to expand as computing power increases and networked image databases expand. While these programs are technologically intriguing and artistically fascinating, they also bring about a number of challenges related to the ethics of copyright and fair use. These are issues that will certainly be relevant to art educators, designers, and media scholars as the 21st century progresses. As the work of Anderson indicates, educators, artists and theorists will need to push back against the techno-deterministic forces that pursue and fund projects such as these. By taking a technological feminist stance (Slotte Dufva, 2023) that is closely related to Feminist New Materialism, the challenges of AI art can be identified and scrutinized.

Another developing practice in contemporary digital visual artistic production related to indeterminate variability is the creation of Non-fungible tokens, or NFT's. NFT's confront aspects of indeterminate variability in curious ways, and it is therefore important that I discuss them here. Although NFT's have been a part of the discussion concerning alternative currencies such as bitcoin since 2012 (Steinwold, 2019), they were introduced to the art market by artist Kevin McCoy in 2015 (Ullman, 2015). But it was the sale of *Everydays: The First 5000 Days* (2019) by the digital artist Beeple that brought

NFT's to prominence, primarily due to its sale at auction for 69 million dollars (Silver, 2021).

NFT's are a unique form of digital art where the history and origin of the work is verifiable through the blockchain. Blockchain technology had also been in existence well before the first NFT artworks were produced. This technology allows for the ownership of the specific NFT to be recorded in a decentralized network, which makes forgery almost impossible. This is the same technology that allows digital currencies such as bitcoin to be exchanged, and for it to gain value. NFT's represent a radical, if somewhat contradictory, shift in notions of uniqueness in digital visual art. All of the work that I have been discussing is informed by the ability for data to be copied, transmuted, and reorganized with ease. This variability is a hallmark of new media art, for example, as Manovich (2000) has argued.

NFT's counter this variability by establishing, in the blockchain, the ability to determine what is the original digital work and what is the copy. Digital visual works of art such as *After Walker Evans* (2001) and *After Sherri Levine* (2001) by Michael Mandiberg leverage the reproducibility of digital images, taking the practices of appropriation used by Sherri Levine into the digital age. These digital readymades were, as the name implies, a rethinking of the artistic strategies of artists such as Marcel Duchamp. NFT's force the rethinking of digital art as inherently replicable, motivated as much by theoretical concerns as by late-stage capitalistic drives. In this manner, NFT's can be considered as post-digital, as they rely upon technologies that are truly contemporary, while at the same time employing market-based tactics that have existed for hundreds of years.

A Digital Visual Art Education must acknowledge the perplexing and problematic aspects of advanced technologies such as AI and NFT's. The concepts of indeterminacy and variability can help with this acknowledgement. Indeterminacy and variability deal with concepts of temporality, materiality, and ethics. The notion of the post-digital challenges the relentless drive toward the new in new media art, by fusing media that is outdated with that which is cutting edge. The socio-critical theories known as Feminist New Materialism complicate previous notions of agency and anthropocentrism that are the bedrock of Western humanist epistemologies. Feminist New Materialism looks at these concepts and introduces a healthy skepticism that can help art, design, and media educators who are navigating new technological terrains. And last the variable nature of digital media art should be scrutinized for its political, ethical, and capitalistic dimensions. The ability for digital visual art to be made and remade again and again should be seen as a political act, while the ability for digital art to be presented as a unique object should be placed into the proper art historical frame. To view such practices as politically or ethically neutral is naïve at best.

To conclude this chapter, I will return to the work of Giertz in order to see if the discussion of post-digital materiality can help us to better understand the compelling aspects of her so-called useless machines, and the potential for indeterminacy and variability in a Digital Visual Art Education. First, the ways of making that Giertz employs are those that are familiar to her. She uses materials that are easily acquired and applied in her robots. The final products are generally raw, and clearly do not work as they are intended. The unrefined, humorous qualities of the works are what seems to make them compelling. Second, Giertz describes herself as a maker. She does not refer to herself as an artist, or a designer, or an engineer. In her 2018 TED talk, she is most energized when she is talking about her ideas for making; indeed, some of her designs seem like they are purely functional, with little attention to the final presentation or the look of the device. In fact, the raw quality of the works related to the concept of the poor image belies the amount of work that each device required.

If Giertz were to have created these useless machines in the space of art, design, or media education they would probably be thought of quite differently. In fact, what seems to be the most compelling aspect of Giertz's work is that it is self-generated. She makes a point to say that she taught herself, representing an individualism that runs through many maker communities. In addition, she makes no specific reference to artists, designers, or engineers in her work. These references could have provided Giertz, and her audience, with a formal understanding of the development of robots, but this is inevitably imposing an educational set of constraints over what was made outside of this environment. It is crucial that interested art, design, and media educators assess the value of makerspaces as related to their practices, while respecting those properties that cannot be translated into the spaces of education.

Art, design, and media educators must also be cognizant of the political nature of the makerspace movement. Makerspaces are often associated with STEM initiatives, which are tied to the world of business and commerce in a very direct manner. Of course, art, design, and media education is no different in this regard. However, the marketing of digital technologies has been commonly linked with a rhetoric of self-empowerment and utopian social development (Sweeny, 2004). Art, design, and media educators can analyze these narratives, helping art students to critique the ways that digital technologies are marketed and promoted. Art educators specifically can contribute to the teaching of technology in makerspaces, because art education can speak to a larger visual cultural context (Freedman, 1997). Design educators can speak to the formal processes of product design, while media educators can speak to the ways that such products are framed through mass marketing and advertising, for example.

This marketing influences every aspect of the makerspace movement, even down to the name makerspace. Calling the use of various technologies in the art classroom a makerspace might allow for some degree of recognition, particularly from other educators who are interested in various aspects of maker culture. However, it might also place an undue burden the use of these technologies. By assuming that all technological activities have something to do with the maker movement, or STEM, or that there is even a measurable educational outcome to be found in these activities, the process of inquiry is guided, at best. At worst, it is stifled.

These are issues that are complicated, to say the least. It is because they are complicated that they should be taken up by art, design, and media educators. It is my hope that, if similar research is undertaken in other fields, by like-minded researchers, artists, scientists, and inquisitive individuals in general, that our understanding of Digital Visual Art Education will be more inclusive, more humorous, and more socially engaging.

I will be discussing further implications for indeterminacy, variability, and post-digital materiality within art, design, and media education in the concluding chapter. Before this takes place, I will outline the third element of a Digital Visual Art Education in Chapter Four: Intersectionality.

References

Anderson, S. (2022). *The Alt-Right Manipulated My Comic. Then A.I. Claimed It.* Accessed January, 2023, from https://www.nytimes.com/2022/12/31/opinion/sarah-andersen-how-algorithim-took-my-work.html

Bajarin, T. (2014). Why the Maker Movement Is Important to America's Future. *Time Magazine*. Retrieved March 2023 from http://time.com/104210/maker-faire-maker-movement/

Barad, K. (2007). *Meeting the Universe Halfway: Quantum Physics and the Entanglement of Matter and Meaning*. Duke University Press.

Bates, K. G. (2016). When It Comes to 'Colored Peoples Time,' Context Matters. *Code Switch*. Retrieved March, 2023, from https://www.npr.org/sections/codeswitch/2016/04/13/474069083/when-it-comes-to-terms-like-colored-peoples-time-context-matters

Brown, J. F. (2015). *Senate ESEA Push Yields Huge Victory for STEM Education*. Retrieved March, 2023, from http://www.stemedcoalition.org/2015/04/21/senate-esea-push-yields-huge-victory-for-stem-education/

Cramer, F. (2014). What Is 'Post-Digital?' *APRJA*, *3*(1).

Dewey, J. (1916). *Democracy and Education*. New York, NY: Macmillan.

Dewey, J. (1937). *Art as Experience*. New York, NY: Norton.

Donnett, N. (2014). About. Retrieved March, 2023, from https://www.nathanieldonnett.com/about

Dougherty, D. (2012). *Makerspaces in Education and DARPA*. Retrieved March 2023 from http://makezine.com/2012/04/04/makerspaces-in-education-and-darpa/

Freedman, K. (2003). *Teaching Visual Culture: Curriculum, Aesthetics, and the Social Life of Art*. Teachers College Press; NAEA Press.

Giertz, S. (2018). Why You Should Make Useless Things. *TED Talk*. Retrieved June, 2022, from https://www.youtube.com/watch?v=c0bsKc4tiuY&t=112s

Goode, L. (2019). Why the 'Queen of Shitty Robots' Renounced Her Crown. *Wired Magazine*. Retrieved June, 2022, from: https://www.wired.com/story/simone-giertz-build-what-you-want/

Halverson, E. R., & Sheridan, K. (2014). The Maker Movement in Education. *Harvard Educational Review*, *84*(4), 495–504.

Klüver, B. (1969). Experiments in Art and Technology. *Members Newsletter, Museum of Modern Art 3*, 4–7. Retrieved from http://www.jstor.org/stable/4380551

Marzio, P. (1972). Art, Technology and Satire: The Legacy of Rube Goldberg. *Leonardo*, *5*(4), 315–324. https://doi.org/10.2307/1572586

Mondloch, K. (2018). *A Capsule Aesthetic: Feminist Materialisms in New Media Art*. University of Minnesota Press.

Papert, S., & Harel, I. (1991). *Constructionism*. New York, NY. Ablex Publishing Corporation.

Peppler, K. (2010). Arts Education for a Digital Age. *Teachers College Record 112*(8), 2118–2153.

Russell, L. (n.d.). *Meet Legacy* (Webpage). Retrieved January, 2023, from https://www.legacyrussell.com/MEET-LEGACY

Sendcindiver, S. Y. (2017). New Materialism. Oxford Bibliographies. Retrieved March, 2023, from https://www.oxfordbibliographies.com/view/document/obo-9780190221911/obo-9780190221911-0016.xml

Silver, N. S. (2021). The History And Future of NFTs. *Forbes Magazine*. Retrieved January, 2023, from https://www.forbes.com/sites/nicolesilver/2021/11/02/the-history-and-future-of-nfts/?sh=f1441e86a163

Slotte Dufva, T. (2023). Entanglements in AI Art. In A. Knochel & O. Sahara (Eds.), *Global Media Arts Education: Mapping Global Perspectives of Media Arts in Education*. Palgrave Macmillan.

Steyerl, H. (2009). In Defense of the Poor Image. *E-flux Journal#10*, Retrieved March, 2023, from https://www.e-flux.com/journal/10/61362/in-defense-of-the-poor-image/

Sweeny, R. (2017). Making and Breaking in an Art Educational Makerspace. In E. Caryannadis (Ed.), *The Journal for Innovation and Entrepreneurship*.

Steinwold, A. (2019). *The History of Non Fungible Tokens*. Retrieved January, 2023, from https://medium.com/@Andrew.Steinwold/the-history-of-non-fungible-tokens-nfts-f362ca57ae10

Thompkins, K. W. (2016). On the Limits and Promise of New Materialist Philosophy. *Lateral: Journal of the Cultural Studies Association*, 5(1). Retrieved March, 2023, from https://csalateral.org/issue/5-1/forum-alt-humanities-new-materialist-philosophy-tompkins/#fnref-363-7

Ullman, S. (2019). *Who Created NFT's?* Accessed February, 2013, from https://www.rarecircles.com/blog/who-created-nfts-complete-history

Varga, J. C., & James, J. A. (2012). Refusing Blackness-as-victimization: Trayvon Martin and the Black Cyborgs. In *Pursuing Trayvon Martin: Historical Contexts and Contemporary Manifestations of Racial Dynamics* (pp. 193–205).

Zhang, J. (2014). Artist Transforms Obsolete Devices into Autonomous Drawing Machines. *My Modern Met*. Retrieved March 2023 from http://mymodernmet.com/echo-yang-autonomousmachines

· 4 ·

INTERSECTIONAL: DIGITAL VISUAL IDENTITY AND DIGITAL VIDEO ART

Many of the digital visual artists that have been previously analyzed share one common trait: the use of the video sharing platform YouTube. YouTube was first launched in 2005, and by the summer of 2006 the site had 13 million unique visitors every day that watched more than a hundred million video clips (Snickars & Vonderau, 2009). It was quickly purchased by Google in October 2006 for 1.65 billion USD (Kim, 2012). Since this time, YouTube has influenced traditional broadcast television, inspiring every major network to either create a unique streaming service, or partner with one in existence. It also initiated strict copyright policies designed to limit the reproduction of copywritten content (Andrejevic, 2009). Proprietary algorithms provide users with suggested videos, which allows YouTube to further develop powerful mechanisms that anticipate user behavior. The specific workings of these algorithms are hidden from the view of the user, which runs counter to the notion of visibility described in my theorization of digital visuality. The reflexivity enabled by these algorithms is also stifled by the lack of transparency in the coding of the platform.

In many ways the relationship between YouTube and traditional broadcast media parallels the relationship between commercial art venues and digital visual art practices. Just as YouTube has remediated broadcast television, digital visual art has changed the way that traditional works of art are made, seen, bought and sold (Kholeif, 2018). Specifically, YouTube has brought together previously separate media, centralizing what was previously distributed:

> ...in our current era of wireless social networking the emphasis is not on radical new forms of mediation but on seamless connectivity, ubiquity, mobility and affectivity. YouTube provides perhaps the paradigmatic instance of this new media formation, insofar as its popularity is less a result of having provided users with new and better forms of media than of making available more mediation events, more easily shared and distributed through e-mail, texting, social networks, blogs or news sites. YouTube is also part and parcel of the proliferation of still and video cameras as standard features of mobile phones and the multiplication and mobilization of social networking, so that 3G phones now routinely carry both cameras and social networks (Grusin, 2009).

It is this consolidation of previous media forms, and the power that comes with them, that seems to contradict the ethos of user accessibility and openness that YouTube was started with. In this quote we can see the variability that was discussed as a component of digital visuality in Chapter One, particularly as Grusin (2009) describes the distribution of media. Ironically, the centralization of media sharing options here seems to run counter to the decentralization that I have been holding up as vital to digital visual works of art.

In 2009 I wrote a piece titled "There's No 'I' in YouTube: Social Media, Networked Identity, and Art Education." In this paper, published in the International Journal of Education Through Art, I proposed that the video sharing site contributed to a contemporary form of identity formation which I termed networked identity. Networked identity represents the fragmentation and dispersion of a central, Modernist artistic persona often displayed in digital visual art (Sweeny, 2009b). Here, I am arguing that digital visual works of art can highlight the ways that identity has been further fragmented, multiplied, and made intersectional through the advances made in digital media. In order to update the concept of networked identity, it is necessary to look more closely at these strategies. Digital visual identity is, as I will propose, a better description of the process by which new media artists such as Wanda Raimundi and Jayson Musson explore and challenge artistic identity.

Wanda Raimundi is an artist who uses a variety of media to explore, expand, and explode aspects of artistic identity. Her "Ask Chuleta" twenty-episode video series is available on YouTube. As she states on her webpage (www.raimundiart.com):

> In the guise of my alter ego, Chuleta, a sassy, no-nonsense NuyoRican art enthusiast became my way of calling out biases of both the art world as well as my own people by becoming a sort of urban art translator, conduit, culture critic, interceptor and interrogator. It was a wild experiment that predates current YouTube styling and confessional style video format designed to breach the art world and reach out beyond the confines of the "white cube" to talk to anyone that wanted to listen.

Raimundi's performances can be understood through the concept of intersectionality. Intersectionality was first theorized by critical race theorist and black feminist legal scholar Kimberlé Crenshaw in 1989, and since that time it has been taken up by numerous theorists and applied to many fields, including art education (Kraehe & Acuff, 2013). Intersectionality is an important analog to how I am theorizing digital visual identity in digital visual art, as it takes into account class, race, and gender, and does so in ways that acknowledge complexity and contradiction. Intersectionality should be considered as a decentralized set of sociocultural influences; there is no one dominant factor, as in a centralized network, nor are all factors equally influential, as in a distributed network. In a decentralized communicational network, hubs form where individual nodes tend to group, and through which messages are channeled.

I am using decentralization to map out relationships that occur within works of digital visual art. I am not specifically speaking to forms of electronic communication, as in the case of researchers such as Baran (1964). I am, instead, using decentralization as a motif, as a model for interpreting and understanding complex relationships, in a manner that is more closely related to the theorization of the rhizome by Deleuze and Guattari (1987). These can be complex relationships between individuals, or they can be complex relationships between materials, or they can extend to power relationships as they exist within and between institutions. I will strive to be as clear as possible as to what type of network I am referencing throughout this text.

We can see intersectionality as it relates to social relationships in Raimundi's statement above, in the passage where Chuleta calls out "biases of both the art world and my own people." Her work is not focused on one topic, or in one form of criticism. Her ability to operate from both within a system and from its margins gives the Chuleta character its particular resonance:

> I find the uncomfortable positions, and I want to stick my finger in and poke fun at the institution that has kept me employed. Initially, that project was inspired by trying to explain my career to a relative about how I can go into a gallery and sit for

> three hours letting people dump trash on me. [It] sounds ridiculous because this job is very weird, so I came up with Chuleta (Pirani, 2016).

The fact that the character was born out of Raimundi's need to explain her art to a family member speaks to a history of performance art, and theatre in general, that draws upon personal experience. It speaks specifically to Schechner's (1990) reading of mimesis, and its relationship to twice-behaved behavior: "Mimesis is a subcategory of twice-behaved behavior where the figure on stage is standing for something else" (p. 98). The ability for artists to operate within and between different persona is, of course, nothing new. However, what is new in this relationship is the impact that digital media can have upon identity. Much has been written on this topic, but for the sake of clarity, I will focus on the reading of digital identity proposed by Sherry Turkle (1995), in order to more fully expand this notion of a digital visual identity.

Life on the Screen: Identity in the Age of the Internet is a landmark work that looks at the sociological implications of computer use. It builds upon Turkle's previous book, The Second Self: Computers and the Human Spirit (1985), which is also considered to be foundational in the study of the psychology of digital technologies. In Life on the Screen, Turkle describes the nascent internet as it was just starting to expand across the globe and intertwine with daily habits and individual subjectivities:

> We come to see ourselves differently as we catch sight of our images in the mirror of the machine… A rapidly expanding system of networks, collectively known as the Internet, links millions of people in new spaces that are changing the way we think, the nature of our sexuality, the form of our communities, our very identities (p. 5).

As Turkle (1995) suggests, a fragmented identity can be seen as abnormal, particularly when read through Psychoanalytic theories of the early to mid-20th century. Unless there is a central core, the notion of the individual begins to break down. Since the publication of Life on the Screen, Turkle has shifted her focus away from a descriptive, anthropological approach, and towards a critical, at times skeptical view of digital technology. As she states:

> I wrote my first book really in an effort to get people like me, humanists and anthropologists and psychologists, to look at these things with an open heart. That was about at the beginning of sociable robotics, the creation of machines that pretended to care about you. That appeared to love you. The other big development was devices with the ability to distract you all the time. I was very positive on the whole about machines that you physically went to. That you had to pull up a chair to. But once

> these things were with you all the time, I really wanted to study how the world changes with that possibility. (Adams, 2015, n.p.)

Her recent work deals with that which is lost when networked digital technologies are central to daily lives and identities. Writing in the same period as Life on the Screen, but from a philosophical perspective, Gilles Deleuze (1992) suggests that a similar breakdown is the result of the forces at play in what he terms "societies of control." In societies of control, the individual is multiplied through the use of digital passwords, codes, and information collected by databases.[1] This process results in a fragmentation of identity, resulting in what Deleuze calls a "dividual:"

> According to Deleuze's explanations in "The Postscripts of the Societies of Control," the disciplinary regime has two poles, in which it is equally interested. It masses together and individualizes, constituting the mass as a body and modularizing its members as individuals… (Raunig, 2016, p. 120)

It is within and between these poles that the dividual is constituted. Raunig (2016) expands and updates this concept, drawing upon the history of the notion of the *dividuum* in order to speak to contemporary digital identity formation. The dividual as identity formation aligns with the deskilling of labor in the digital economy:

> Crowds, multitudes, dispersed masses—their modes of existence and living are captured, stretched, appropriated and exploited beyond the realm of paid labor. Scoring, rating, ranking, profiling. Consumers who are activated and generate value with their activity do not have to be paid. The open source model of program development by the crowd has meanwhile become established as a business model and spread to all economic sectors. Free labor in free association, but to the advantages of the New Economy (p. 124).

This brings us back to the history of YouTube, and the dynamics of sharing that were initially promoted on the site. The ability to upload personal videos was only one component of the original site. Once videos were uploaded, they could be viewed, liked or disliked, and shared. This interactive model helped to standardize these actions for the majority of social media platforms that would follow YouTube, as Grusin (2009) states. They also provided the owners of the sites access to a vast amount of behavioral data on who was watching, what they were watching, and who they were watching with:

> One of the advantages of an interactive platform for the delivery of commercial content is that it enables the capture of increasingly detailed information about patterns of user behavior and response. Interactive marketers envision not just the ability to target users based on an expanding range of information about their backgrounds, tastes and behavior, but also the ability to conduct ongoing controlled experiments to determine which forms of consumer inducement are most effective in managing and channeling audience behavior. (Andrejevic, 2009)

This description of dataveillance as it is enabled through YouTube usage fits within the societies of control as theorized by Deleuze (1992). In Chapter One I was emphasizing the ways that societies of control might use visuality to view and limit social behaviors. Here I am looking to the relationship between these societies as theorized by Deleuze as they relate to identity as it is framed through digital platforms such as YouTube. Deleuze was not able to foresee specific aspects of such systems; specifically, the monetization of such participatory networked spaces. Where Deleuze and Raunig offers a warning regarding the intersections of interactive technologies and identity, Turkle (1995) suggests an active form of deterritorialization can be seen in the use of networked technologies. She suggests that the homepage is an apt model for the center of the fragmented self, though she was writing before the turn of the 21st century.

Writing about networked identity in 2009, I suggested the following:

> … in an age of social media, the center for networked identity resides not in a distinct, potentially isolated homepage, but is distributed throughout the social networking sites such as Facebook or MySpace. These sites aggregate information from various Internet locations and comprise the online identity of the user in the process. Identity is found in the relationships between the sites, as well as how they interconnect, or fail to do so, with lived experience. Moreover, the networked identity of the user is intertwined with the identity of his or her friends, coworkers, family, and perhaps total strangers (Sweeny, 2009).

This dynamic process has only expanded since this was originally written. As we have seen, corporations such as YouTube continue to contribute to the networked identities composed within a digital visual culture. While there are aspects to this process that are worthy of caution, such as in cases of identity theft and datamining there are also possibilities for the exploration of new identities, which can be particularly potent when folded back into everyday interactions. It is this expanded network of interactions that I am calling digital visual identity, as the previous notion of networked identity was not specific enough. There are different types of networks, and the type that is most closely related to the identities that are formed through digital media are of the decentralized type.

Digital Visual Identity and Digital Visual Art

The persona of Hennessy Youngman created by Jayson Musson speaks to, and about, issues of representation and race in the artworld. The relationship between Musson and Youngman begins to expand our understanding of his identity, but this binary is only the start. In most videos, Musson/Youngman greets the viewer, and then introduces himself, stating the name of his persona, and then listing additional names: "What up internet? It's your boy Hennessey Youngman, aka Henrock Obama aka The Pharaoh Hennessey" (Musson, 2011). Many people have used pseudonyms, from actors to authors to politicians to gangsters to artists. In Musson's case, this seems to be a particular reference to rappers, based upon frequent references to hip hop in his work: "Hip-hop is an intrinsic part of my language. So you are always going to utilize this primary language that you have" (Iadarola, 2018). Rappers are known to use a variety of pseudonyms, changing names when they change styles. (Phillips, 2018)

This play with naming fits within the theory of digital visual identity that I am presenting in this chapter. In terms of the notion of the dividual, Musson/Youngman's many personae make reference to the fragmentation that is central to identity, outside of the influence of databases and electronic networks. However, because they use YouTube as a platform, the digital sphere must be acknowledged in relation to this division. As previously discussed, Raimundi/Chuleta spoke to viewers through two specific platforms: YouTube and art spaces/galleries. Musson/Youngman also speaks through these platforms. It is hard to know the nature of the audience who views their YouTube videos. However, in an interesting twist to this anonymity, YouTube viewership is painstakingly quantified, as all views are monitored and measured, as Andrejevic (2009) suggests.

It is much easier to identify the audience who visits art galleries: art viewers. This seems simplistic, and somewhat tautological, but is it a useful distinction. Both Raimundi/Chuleta and Musson/Youngman are speaking to a knowing audience when their videos are displayed within an art space. As Musson states: "The Hennessey project is successful, in like an artworld sense, because in some way I think Hennessey fulfills this narcissistic desire of the artworld to want to hear about itself and hear about itself in a new language" (2012). Language is central to the work of both Raimundi/Chuleta and Musson/Youngman. Both speak directly to the viewer, in a confessional manner that has become very common on YouTube. In writing about Musson's work, Iadarola (2018) states:

> From the style of plain-spoken, at times risqué gallows humor he perfected to the ways in which the project was designed for widespread informal dissemination—sidestepping institutional gatekeeping in the process—the work is almost uncanny in its prescience of the current moment. Additionally, it engaged the affective dimension of what Hito Steyerl has called "poor images" while anticipating the contemporary omnipresence of what Manuel Arturo Abreu has called Online Imagined Black English, or digital blackface (n.p.).

These two concepts will be helpful for the discussion of digital visual identity. First, I will discuss Abreu's theory of Online Imagined Black English as it relates more closely to the issue of language as it is being discussed. Online Imagined Black English was developed by Abreu in their essay of the same name. In this essay, Abreu describes the appropriation of Black culture as it relates to digital forms of expression, placing it within a history that dates back to the era of slavery in the United States. As is commonly known, whites in this era wore blackface in performances intended to degrade and humiliate Blacks. The legacy of blackface has endured, becoming a central component of popular visual culture as described by Williams-Witherspoon (2013): "The vanguards of white American popular culture reframes stereotypes and the 'performance of blackness'; and then commodifies it in wholesale terms under the rubric of 'nationalism', as indigenous manifestations of American culture." (p. 2)

As the history of minstrelsy shows, Black as well as white performers were enlisted to perform in blackface, which speaks to the complicated nature of what Musson is performing through the persona of Hennessey Youngman. When Youngman speaks in the language of contemporary hip-hop, he is, as Iadarola (2018) suggests, "anticipating the omnipresence" of this language. In other words, Youngman is making a statement on the absence of Black artists in contemporary art circles through language that has been appropriated to the point where it is ubiquitous.

In his exploration of "digital blackface," Abreu references the work of linguist William Labov (1972), who theorized that language changes from the bottom up and from the top down and is most influenced by upwardly mobile women. He called this theory the "Gender Paradox:"

> A standard network-theoretic explanation of the gender paradox is as follows: men's networks are more densely clustered and local, regional, nonstandard, and resistant to change; women's networks, on the other hand, tend to be more open and less local, leading to more access to innovative forms as well as a greater tendency to adopt non-regional standard variants. (Abreu, n.d.)

This network-theoretic explanation fits within the theory of digital visual identity that I am developing in this chapter. As Abreu describes, the decentralized network represented by women's networks is more open to change than the centralized networks found in men's social spheres.

Steyerl's (2009) "poor image" can be helpful when discussing many of the artists who use YouTube as a platform to play with and problematize identity. The "poor image" demonstrates the following characteristics: It is of low resolution; it represents the resurrection of previous media; it threatens neoliberal privatization as it is also taken up in capitalist networks of dissemination. The YouTube works of Raimundi/Chuleta and Musson/Youngman speak to each of these characteristics. First, they create video works that are deliberately of low quality. Both use smartphone cameras to record and upload, with what seems to be very little editing involved. The Musson/Youngman pieces include title sequences and theme music; the sequences are deliberately crude, and the music is typically hip-hop. Both speak in a manner that seems unrehearsed, which adds to the directness of the performances. Second, both artists take part in practices that are common within previous artistic traditions. However, these practices, whether they be the performative personae of Guillermo Gomez-Pena or the photographic variations presented by Cindy Sherman, were generally contained within the gallery/museum system. Raimundi/Chuleta and Musson/Youngman operate in these closed, centralized systems, as well as the considerably more distributed networks of YouTube. Third, and related to the last point, Raimundi/Chuleta and Musson/Youngman operate between forces of commercialism and subversion. This is the aspect that is most closely related to the notion of digital visual identity that I am developing. On this point, Steyerl (2009) states:

> The networks in which poor images circulate thus constitute both a platform for a fragile new common interest and a battleground for commercial and national agendas. They contain experimental and artistic material, but also incredible amounts of porn and paranoia. While the territory of poor images allows access to excluded

> imagery, it is also permeated by the most advanced commodification techniques. While it enables the users' active participation in the creation and distribution of content, it also drafts them into production. Users become the editors, critics, translators, and (co-)authors of poor images (n.p.).

Much has been written on shifts in the traditional producer/consumer dyad that were established in previous media forms. Though this topic is beyond the scope of this chapter, it is relevant to mention the way that YouTube allows for, and in fact encourages viewer participation in the form of liking videos, and subscribing to content producer channels, as Raunig (2016) describes.

In addition to these aspects of the "poor image," I would like to include an additional interpretation as the concept relates to the work of Raimundi/Chuleta and Musson/Youngman. Both make a number of references to socioeconomic class in their performances. For Musson/Youngman there is an assumed tension between the streetwise Youngman and the Ivy League-educated Musson. However, if read through the lens of intersectionality, then this binary is troubled. Could it not be the case that one who speaks and dresses like Youngman attends The University of Pennsylvania? This is a trap that journalists have fallen into, as Syms (2016) points out:

> Some viewers mistake his black mask for a face, like journalist Dan Duray, who write a problematic feature on Musson with the clickbait title: 'Henny from the block: Jayson Musson is not an idiot, he just plays one on YouTube.' In the profile, Duray critiques Youngman's excessiveness, calling the cadence 'over the top thug speak.' Duray also comments on Musson's real speaking voice which (according to him) 'sounds like Hennessey imitating a white person,' and notes that Musson self-identifies as 'West Indian.' (p. 379)

The slippages between Musson and Youngman open up spaces for the questioning of identity in general, and in this case identity as it relates to class and race. What is interesting is that, in this description of his work, the medium is never discussed. The poor image, is perhaps, so poor as to be discounted altogether.

In the case of Raimundi/Chuleta, the issue of socioeconomic class is often mentioned. She often speaks to her attire and her hair in the videos and makes a point to try to communicate directly to her viewers, explaining theoretical art terms and concepts for them. In her second video, she is promoting an exhibition at Longwood Gallery in the Bronx, NYC: "I know y'all be moaning and groaning: 'I gotta pay the bills. I gotta pay the rent. Yo. It's free. Ain't got no excuse" (2009). She goes on to provide more details about the show, including the name of the curator, who is Wanda Ortiz. This playful reference is, once again, a nod to the slippage regarding identity in her work. In fact, she references "Wanda Ortiz" here, while her YouTube page lists "Wanda Raimundi Ortiz" as the creator of content. Her website states her name as "Wanda Raimundi." Who is the artist? Does each name represent a different approach to artmaking? Has her name changed over time? Is this simply a decision that she has made to present herself in three different ways, or is this an extension of her explorations of identity? In keeping with the intersectional aspects of digital visual identity, it is potentially a bit of both.

As in the case of Musson/Youngman, Raimundi/Chuleta is using an accessible medium to speak to and raise issues about class. The smartphone video, uploaded to YouTube with minimal edits speaks to authenticity. But is it authentic? Surely one could argue that web videos produced under a pseudonym are not. But within the parameters of a digital visual culture, one might not be so sure of this conclusion. Digital visual identity brings with it a level of uncertainty. Who is the speaker? Who is the audience? Along with the questions that digital visual identity raises comes the question of authenticity and value. In many artistic traditions, cultural and monetary value is bestowed upon the unique object, as Walter Benjamin famously argued in The Work of Art in the Age of Mechanical Reproduction (1968). With YouTube the shift from a user-generated focus to a corporate profit-making platform has raised a host of issues including but not limited to originality and commodity. A Marxist analysis of content production sheds some light on the connections between YouTube and previous media forms, while it also leads to further questions. Andrejevic (2009) speaks to the role that the YouTube content creator plays in this capitalist framework:

> As a condition of their "free" acquiescence to engage in this productive exchange, they both construct popular websites and submit to the forms of monitoring and experimentation that are becoming an integral component of the interactive economy. Their free participation is redoubled as a form of productive labor captured by capital—and the offer to overcome estrangement or alienation produces a second-order form of separation between uses and "cybernetic commodities" they generate about their social lives: their behavior; their tastes, preferences, patterns of consumption and response to advertising. It is in this regard that the frequent invocations of women's historical role in the production of affective or immaterial labor become germane: women's domestic labor in the era of industrial production is also unwaged, and yet provided under conditions shaped by the forcible separation of the means of production from workers. (pp. 419–420)

Neither Raimundi/Chuleta and Musson/Youngman have monetized their YouTube channels as numerous social media influencers have. Nor have they participated in the exploitation that Andrejevic describes above. Again, they play between the poles of monetization and exploitation, in a decentralized manner. One assumes that they have been able to use the relative success of their YouTube channels to assist entry into gallery and museum exhibitions, and perhaps the collections of private art collectors.

The quote from Andrejevic indicates one very important aspect of digital visual identity that is related to intersectionality: capitalist processes are always tied to forms of gender identification. Throughout this chapter, I have been discussing the work of Musson/Youngman, who identifies as male, and Raimundi/Chuleta, who identifies as female. I am basing this identification upon their individual forms of self-presentation: both make reference to traditional gender in their clothing, hairstyles, and adornments such as jewelry. They also refer to their own gender in their videos, which is undoubtedly referencing the characters that they are presenting. Both characters present an exaggerated sense of masculinity/femininity, which is surely related to the performance of gender on YouTube in general.

Raimundi/Chuleta makes numerous references to gender presentation in her videos, usually in regard to her personal appearance in the *Ask Chuleta* series. In 2011 she created an offshoot series, titled *Doobie Culture*, where she discusses "fashion, culture, and love:" "Ladies, I want to see you post pictures, take pictures of your best doobie game. Yo, I want to see pinches, I want to see pouts, and I want to see pantallas." In this passage, Chuleta makes reference to hairclips, lipstick, and earrings, using terms that are specific to Puerto Rican dialects, which speaks to the aspects of language that are important to consider when discussing decentralized identity in digital visual art.

Musson/Youngman also makes frequent references to gender in his *Art Thoughtz* series. One very clear reference to gender as it relates to the contemporary artworld can be found in the episode titled "How To Be A Successful Artist." In this episode, which is the first in the *Art Thoughtz* series, he lists the criteria necessary to reach the titular goal:

> First, be white. Being white helps in the artworld, 'cause I don't know. White makes the world go around… Two: Be a white male. If you are a white man, pretty much your voice is the universal voice. Therefore anything you make won't be burdened by any sort of cultural label that [n-word] and [b-word] have to deal with… [Three] Be a white woman. This way you could put on a wig. You could explore identity through

> your wig. 'Cause you know, it's rough not having a dick. And lord knows it's rough being a woman in the Sudan, I mean America (2011)

Although his language might be considered coarse by some standards, the intersection of gender discrimination and racial discrimination that Youngman identifies is backed up by recent research. As reported by Kinsella (2019):

> Researchers examined more than 40,000 artworks in the collections of 18 museums across the US, including the Metropolitan Museum of Art in New York, the Detroit Institute of Arts, and the Art Institute of Chicago, to analyze the gender and ethnic diversity of their holdings. They estimate that 85 percent of artists represented in these collections are white and 87 percent are men. (This is, notably, significantly out of step with the US population at large, which is 61 percent white and 50.2 percent male, according to census data.)

At this point it is necessary to review the aspects of digital visual identity that have been discussed, so that I can clarify the relevance of this concept for art, design, and media educators. Again, my thesis is that digital visual art can help to identify and perhaps better understand these aspects of digital visual identity as they relate to a Digital Visual Art Education.

Digital Visual Identity and Individuality

The first aspect of digital visual identity that I will discuss is related to the notion of the individual, or more specifically, the breakdown of the individual in contemporary society that Deleuze (1992) termed the "dividual." The "dividual" was theorized by Deleuze (1992) in his essay Postscripts on the Societies of Control. In this essay, Deleuze builds upon the work of Foucault, who spoke to the parameters of disciplinary societies and the control that they exert over the individual in Discipline and Punish: The Birth of the Prison (1975). For Deleuze, the enclosures that Foucault analyzes are in a state of upheaval, as disciplinary societies have led to societies of control, which exert force over its subjects not through distinct systems, but through continual modulation:

> In the societies of control, on the other hand, what is important is no longer either a signature or a number, but a code: the code is a password, while on the other hand the disciplinary societies are regulated by watchwords (as much from the point of view of integration as from that of resistance). The numerical language of control is made of

> codes that mark access to information, or reject it. We no longer find ourselves dealing with the mass/individual pair. Individuals have become "dividuals," and masses, samples, data, markets, or "banks" (p. 5).

This is where the importance of the notion of the "dividual" as related to digital visual identity in digital visual art can be identified. The societies of control scramble previously stable binary relationships such as the mass versus the individual. Instead there is a distribution of power that spreads across these previously distinct forms of identification, and as power shifts from state or private control to that of capitalistic market control. In this distribution, models of interaction and communication shift from centralized to decentralized. Art is caught up in this scenario, according to Deleuze: "Even art has left the spaces of enclosure in order to enter into the open circuits of the bank" (p. 6).

The emphasis in this quote indicates that art, for Deleuze, holds a unique space that has historically been outside of market forces. Regardless of the truth of this, it is important to note that Deleuze had always looked to the arts as he developed his philosophical theories, from literature and poetry to visual art. The world that Deleuze describes in Postscripts on the Societies of Control is rather bleak by most measures. The totalizing effects that he describes seem to offer no options for alternate ways of being, not even through engagement with works of art. Raunig (2016), in response to Deleuze, sees an opportunity for new forms of resistance within the societies of control, in what he calls the General Intellect:

> New challenges emerge when the position of the General Intellect, of a mass, multiple and militant intellectuality, is negotiated today. The intellect that does not close itself off in the single author-individual, the intellect that does not sublate the flows of social knowledge in a communitarian, general, universal unity, invents itself in machinic capitalism as a transversal intellect. This intellect is transversal, because it emerges in traversing the singularities of thinking, speaking, writing, fabricating knowledge: a machinic-dividual stream of thinking that moves across the dichotomy of individual and community, permeates individuals and collectives, inhabits the spaces, things, landscapes between them and allows new forms of disobedience to emerge, new forms of noncompliance, new dissemblages (p. 19)

Although Raunig does not speak specifically to the role that art can play in this emergent situation, his description of the General Intellect here may provide us with an important perspective on the digital visual art practices of Raimundi/Chuleta and Musson/Youngman. Both examples challenge the "single author individual" using language and visual signifiers to create idiosyncratic forms of artistic expression. They do not speak directly to the aspects of the societies of control that rely upon "masses, samples, data, or markets." However, they both channel these forces through their videos, which are presented on YouTube, a platform that relies heavily on such metrics. Digital visual artists using contemporary digital platforms such as YouTube participate in these processes, knowingly or not. What artists such as Raimundi/Chuleta and Musson/Youngman can do is scramble the forms of interaction that they enable. As Syms (2015) writes: "Musson's YouTube activity prompts a deluge of hateful comments that he responds to in character. His voicing of an absent figure invites a slippage between Musson and Youngman" (p. 379). Extending this slippage into the interactions with YouTube viewers is a way for Musson/Youngman to leverage the fragmentation represented by the dividual in his digital visual art.

Digital Visual Identity and Race

The second aspect of digital visual identity that I will discuss relates to race. This seems to be an obvious comparison to make, as race and identity are often very closely aligned. As previously discussed, Abreu's (n.d.) theory of Online Imagined Black English has particular significance when considering the way that language relates to ethnic identity. As previously mentioned, the theory of Online Imagined Black English describes the history of Black cultural appropriation since the era of slavery in the US. As Abreu states:

> The internet allows for communication and media dissemination to a wider and more diffuse audience than was once possible: individuals and communities with less and less relationship to black media and linguistic behavior have access to it, with Urban Dictionary and Genius (formerly Rap Genius) only a few clicks away to provide "definitions." These conditions potentially alter or accelerate the process of deracialization by which words enter standard English, as well as provide more contexts for the performance of racist stereotypes. (n.p.)

The argument that the internet facilitates, and indeed exacerbates racist cultural impulses runs counter to the early descriptions of the internet as a utopian space, free from bias. A critique of this perpetuation of racist forms of appropriation is central to the work of both Raimundi/Chuleta and Musson/Youngman.

Abreu describes the dynamic linguistic qualities of Imagined Black English using the term "code switching:"

> Imagined Black English is an instance of code-switching… Research on code-switching in computer-mediated communication tends to draw on frameworks developed for analyzing spoken, face-to-face discourse…. Online talk is largely text-based, and may follow different sets of norms, particularly in more casual digital contexts such as chat.

Code switching is a term drawn from the linguistic study of bilingual communication. It was originally described in the mid-20th century as the transfer of words, and its importance was downplayed (Gardner-Chloros, 2009). As Abreu indicates, the appropriation of Black vernacular language by non-blacks online is complicated by the difference between spoken language, usually in video form, and text-based communication.

Both Raimundi/Chuleta and Musson/Youngman use vernacular language in their video works: Musson/Youngman draws from hip-hop, while Raimundi/Chuleta incorporates Spanish words that are specific to her Puerto Rican heritage. In this sense, they are not code-switching within the characters of Youngman and Chuleta. Each persona uses a consistent vocabulary and form of presentation. As Syms (2016) writes of Musson/Youngman: "He uses dialect to take control of art world discourse. He refuses to code-switch. He keeps the act in mixed company, whether speaking at a museum or in an interview with Art in America" (p. 386). It is only when they step out of character, where in interviews or artist statements, that they switch to a different form of presentation. This presentation is best described as academic, as both are involved in academic circles. In their videos, both make frequent references to terms drawn from academic art theory, and both make it clear that they are attempting to translate these theories for their viewing audiences. In this manner, both act as a form of teacher. It is not far-fetched to see both Raimundi/Chuleta and Musson/Youngman as engaging in a form of pedagogy.

Language as related to race, in this general sense, always serves to make connections: connections between speaker and viewer, between teacher and learner. Communities are often built and maintained through language that is taught in direct and indirect ways. What happens in the process of the Youngman and Chuleta performances is that their specific use of language points out the gaps between speaker and viewer. If we return to the electronic communication originally theorized by Baran (1964), communicational networks always incorporate a level of noise. The model of the decentralized network allows for messages to be rerouted around disruptions. However, in the case of Raimundi/Chuleta and Musson/Youngman, the disruptions are a part of what is being communicated. Language is always partial, always contains noise. The work of digital visual artists such as Raimundi/Chuleta and Musson/Youngman can help to point to these moments as productive.

Digital Visual Identity and Class

The third aspect of decentralized identity that I will discuss is related to the operations of contemporary capitalism and class. It is clear in the 21st century that capitalism has a profound influence on almost every aspect of culture. Globalism has spread capitalist markets and forms of interaction across the globe, flattening what was once a varied terrain, as Thomas Freedman has argued. And although this flattening is far from ubiquitous, contemporary art markets and modes of distribution have helped to create new art centers across the globe, with Biennials and art fairs emerging in major cities.

Social media networks are a central component of the globalization of capitalism. As previously discussed, YouTube is a particularly robust platform for peer-to-peer sharing and content creation that also raises issues of exploitation of "free" labor (Andrejevic, 2009). Shifts in media forms beginning in the 1970's questioned previous distinctions between producer and consumer, leading to such concepts as the prosumer (Toffler, 1980). Contemporary media further unsettles these binary relationships, to the point where, for example, individuals are required to indicate that they are advertising products on personal social media sites. The homepage that Sherry Turkle saw as the center of digital identity could now, simultaneously, be selling you skin cream or power tools.

In terms of digital visual art, the notion of the "poor image" can provide a useful framework for further analysis of the specific influence of capital and class. As theorized by Steyerl (2009), the "poor image" is specific to digital visual culture and can be understood through three main qualities. First, it is a low-resolution image. Second, it represents the resurrection of previous media. And third, it threatens neoliberal privatization as it is also taken up in capitalist networks of dissemination.

As I have previously discussed, the YouTube works of Raimundi/Chuleta and Musson/Youngman each exhibit these qualities, in varying degrees and in unique ways. Here, I will focus on the third quality, as it speaks directly to the concept of digital visual identity as it relates to digital visual art. Steyerl (2009) describes this quality as such: "The circulation of poor images feeds into both capitalist media assembly lines and alternative audiovisual economies. In addition to a lot of confusion and stupefaction, it also possibly creates disruptive movements of thought and affect" (n.p.). I have already pointed out that digital visual works of art can be used to critique the networks within which they operate, as they simultaneously benefit from the process. I have discussed how the work of Raimundi/Chuleta and Musson/Youngman presents such movements of thought and affect. It is specifically the aspects of individuality and language that are disrupted through the performance-based YouTube video works that I have discussed.

Individuality is disrupted in these works through the use of pseudonym as well as visual signifiers that relate to gender and class. Language is disrupted through references to hip hop and street slang, in the case of Musson/Youngman, and to Puerto Rican Spanish terms in the case of Raimundi/Chuleta. Here, it should be noted that I am focusing on the formal qualities of the work: The name of the artist, the visual signifiers that they include, as well as the language that they use. It is here, at the level of a formal analysis of digital visual art, that we can begin to see the nodes of a digital visual identity forming. Steyerl's emphasis on form might seem odd, as much new media art theory emphasizes sociocultural aspects. However, we must attend to the formal qualities of digital visual art, even though it might seem retrograde.

In addition, I must acknowledge that not all works of digital visual art make use of the poor image. The utility of the concept is, instead, what it can tease out of a variety of digital visual images. The poor image haunts the slick, high-tech world of digital imagery in a post-digital manner, threatening to break the illusion that these images are built upon. Steyerl addresses this world, which she represents through the "rich image:" "The rich image established its own set of hierarchies, with new technologies offering more and more possibilities to creatively degrade it" (n.p.). In this manner, we can see that the concept of the poor image is built upon a binary. It is this binary that is, however, drawn into question by the poor image.

Digital visual identity as it relates to Digital Visual Art Education is built upon images. These images are unstable when compared to the forms of visual identity from the past. Self-portraits, photographs, ID cards, and the like all served to provide a fixed sense of self for the subject who has access to these forms of representation. As Deleuze (1992) pointed to, identity in a digital age is more likely to be found in passcodes and biometric information rather than photographs. As discussed in Chapter One, *Eyes* (2018) is a work by Yoon Chung Han that speaks to this contemporary shift: "The phenomenon of biometric data abuse causes one to question what the notion of 'real' identity means and what methods can be used to define identity and hidden narratives. (n.p.)" DNA samples would be a current way that identity is formed which is related to this notion, in a biometric manner. The popular PBS television show Finding Your Roots with Henry Louis Gates Jr. uses a predictable formula to discuss identity. Participants on the show take time to talk to Gates as they look over family photographs and government documents. Then, in a predictable twist, Gates shares DNA information that points to unseen ethnic influences and, in many cases, the long-lasting and devastating effects of the US slave trade. Here, the science is the truth, and the photos are merely placeholders for hard evidence regarding identity. One can of course purchase this information through companies that offer to provide this data, such as 23 and Me. In an age of social media and late-stage capitalism, identity is yet another commodity that is fluid; as a commodity it can be traded, bought and sold, as Keith Obadike explored in his 2001 work, titled *Blackness for Sale*.[2]

Digital Visual Identity and Gender

The fourth aspect of decentralized identity that I will discuss is related to gender. Gender is central to the contemporary concept of identity, as are concerns regarding individuality, race, and class. Contemporary theories of gender identification and formation challenge biological essentialism, as argued most notably by Judith Butler (1990). Butler argues that gender is performed, and in these performances the binary categories of man and woman are troubled. Many artists have drawn from Butler's work to question and subvert traditional gender distinctions, primarily in the areas of performance art as well as drag performances. It is my contention that our current understanding of gender can be expanded and perhaps further scrutinized through the study of digital visual artists such as Raimundi/Chuleta and Musson/Youngman.

Gender, in these examples, is performed by the titular characters in a manner that allows for self-reflection. Youngman performs a boastful, hypermasculinity in his discussions of contemporary art, while Chuleta is, perhaps equally as boastful, but with an emphasis upon sharing rather than explaining. Labov (1972) theorized that language changes from the bottom up and from the top down, and is most influenced by upwardly mobile women. He called this theory the "Gender Paradox:"

As Abreu describes, the decentralized network represented by women's networks is more open to change than the centralized networks found in men's social spheres. There is an additional element of difference in the self-presentation of Raimundi/Chuleta and Musson/Youngman that relates to the contemporary notion of "mansplaining." Mansplaining is commonly defined as the act of a man explaining something to a woman in a condescending manner. Though the term is the product of late 20th century social media, it has roots that date back to the very beginnings of patriarchy (Rothman, 2012). Musson, in character as Youngman, takes it upon himself to explain the nuances of contemporary art to his viewers. His insight is exaggerated for comedic effect, and though it might not be the main point of the web series, the hypermasculine impact of Youngman's "Art Thoughtz" is hard to miss.

The aspects of gender that are most relevant to digital visual identity are located at the level of the individual, or dividual, and also at the level of sociocultural identification. This is related to Raunig's (2016) description of the societies of control, where the disciplinary regime "masses together and individualizes, constituting the mass as a body and modularizing its members as individuals…" (p. 120). First, the understanding of gender at the level of the individual in contemporary societies is becoming more and more nuanced, with the general acceptance of gender nonconformity and nonbinary forms of identification. This is certainly akin to the decentralized networks that I have been discussing. At the social level, gender continues to be the subject of concern form those who are invested in equal rights for all. Here, the network is shown to be more centralized, with those identifying as male making up the majority of those in positions of power. Smith-Lovin and McPherson (1993) propose a network approach to gender and argue that network analysis can show how social influences create and maintain gender differences. Building from this theory, I am suggesting that the analysis of digital visual art through a network approach can allow for a better understanding of the complexities of contemporary gender identity.

Each of these aspects of identity—individualism, race, class, and gender—can be read through the dynamic structure of the interconnected decentralized network. In this chapter thus far I have shown that digital visual art presents these aspects in unique and provocative ways. Specifically, the YouTube-based work of Raimundi/Chuleta and Musson/Youngman speaks to the complexities of identity in a digital visual culture. In the next chapter I will continue to explore digital visuality through the fourth, and last, component of a Digital Visual Art Education: Interactivity.

Notes

1 In Chapter One, I discussed this essay as it relates to dataveillance and decentralized visuality.
2 I have analyzed this work in detail, in Dysfunction and Decentralization in New Media Art and Education (2015).

References

Adams, T. (2015). Interview: Sherry Turkle: 'I am not anti-technology, I am pro-conversation'. *The Guardian*. Retrieved from https://www.theguardian.com/science/2015/oct/18/sherry-turkle-not-anti-technology-pro-conversation.

Andrejevic, M. (2009). Exploiting YouTube: Contradictions of User-Generated Labor. In P. Snickars & P. Vonderau (Eds.), *The YouTube Reader* (pp. 406–423). Stockholm: The National Library of Sweden.

Baran, P. (1964). On Distributed Communications Networks. *IEEE Transactions of the Professional Technical Group on Communication Systems*, *CS-12*(1). RAND Corporation.

Benjamin, W. (1968). *The Work of Art in the Age of Mechanical Reproduction* (Harry Zohn, Trans.). In Illuminations (H. Arendt, Ed.). New York: Schocken Books.

Crenshaw, K. (1989). *Demarginalizing the Intersection of Race and Sex: Black Feminist Critique of Antidiscrimination Doctrine, Feminist Theory and Antiracist Politics* (pp. 139–168). University of Chicago Legal Forum.

Deleuze, G. (1992). *Postscript on the Societies of Control* (pp. 3–7). October 59. MIT Press.

Foucault, M. (1975). *Discipline and Punish: The Birth of the Prison*. Random House.

Freedman, T. (2005). *The World Is Flat: A Brief History of the 21st Century*. Farrar, Straus and Giroux.

Gardner-Chloros, P. (2009). *Code-Switching*. Cambridge University Press.

Grusin, R. (2009). YouTube at the End of New Media. In P. Snickars & P. Vonderau, (Eds.), *The YouTube Reader*. Stockholm: The National Library of Sweden.

Iadarola, A. (2018). *What Up Internet? Jayson Musson's Art Thoughtz*. Retrieved from https://rhizome.org/editorial/2018/jan/12/what-up-internet/

Kholeif, O. (2018). *Goodbye World! Looking at Art in the Digital Age*. Sternberg Press.

Kim, J. (2012). The Institutionalization of YouTube: From User-Generated Content to Professionally Generated Content. *Media, Culture & Society*, 34(1), 53–67. https://doi.org/10.1177/0163443711427199

Kinsella, E. (2019). An Estimated 85 Percent of Artists Represented in US Museum Collections Are White, a New Study Claims. *Net Art News*. Retrieved from https://news.artnet.com/market/new-study-shows-us-art-museums-grappling-with-diversity-1467256

Kraehe, A., & Acuff, J. (2013). Theoretical Considerations for Art Education Research with and About 'Underserved Populations'. *Studies in Art Education*, 54(4), 294–309. Retrieved from http://www.jstor.org/stable/24465516

Labov, W. (1972). *Language in the Inner City: Studies in the Black English Vernacular*. U. Pennsylvania Press.

Phillips, Y. (2018). *Pseudonyms, Alter Egos, and SEX: Hip Hop's Obsession with Changing Names*. Retrieved from https://djbooth.net/features/2018-02-23-hip-hop-name-changes

Pirani, J. (2016). *All Hail the Queen. Artborne Magazine: Orlando Art and Culture*. Retrieved from http://artbornemagazine.com/all-hail-the-queen/

Raunig, G. (2016). *Dividuum: Machinic Capitalism and Molecular Revolution*. Semiotext(e).

Rothman, L. (2012, November 1). A Cultural History of Mansplaining. *The Atlantic*. Retrieved from https://www.theatlantic.com/sexes/archive/2012/11/a-cultural-history-of-mansplaining/264380/

Schechner, R. (1990). Behavior, Performance, and Performance Space. Perspecta, *Theater, Theatricality, and Architecture*, 26, 97–102.

Smith-Lovin, L., & McPherson, J. (1993). You Are Who You Know: A Network Approach to Gender. In *Theory on Gender: Feminism on Theory* (P. England, Ed., pp. 223–250) Transaction.

Snickars, P., & Vonderau, P. (2009). *The YouTube Reader* (P. Snickars & P. Vonderau, Eds., pp. 9–21). Stockholm: The National Library of Sweden.

Steyerl, H. (2009). In Defense of the Poor Image. *E-flux Journal#10*. https://www.e-flux.com/journal/10/61362/in-defense-of-the-poor-image/

Sweeny, R. (2009). There's No 'I' in YouTube: Social Media, Networked Identity and Art Education. *International Journal of Education through Art*, 5(2) and 3 Article. Intellect.

Sweeny, R. (2015). *Dysfunction and Decentralization in New Media Art and Education*. London, UK: Intellect Press.

Syms, M. (2015). Stages of Laughter 3. *ARTNews*. Accessed online at https://www.artnews.com/art-in-america/features/stages-of-laughter-3-martine-syms-63089/

Toffler, A. (1980). *The Third Wave*. Bantam.

Turkle, S. (1985). *The Second Self: Computers and the Human Spirit*. MIT Press.

Turkle, S. (1995). *Life on the Screen: Identity in the age of the Internet*. New York: Simon and Schuster.

Williams-Witherspoon, K. (2013). Blacks on Stage: Are We Still Replicating Stereotypes from the Legacy of Minstrelsy. *Praxis: The Journal for Theatre, Performance Studies, and Criticism* (1). Retrieved from https://praxis.journals.villanova.edu/article/view/1425

· 5 ·

INTERACTIVE: DIGITAL PLAY AND VIDEOGAMES

In this chapter I will turn to a discussion of interactivity and modes of digital play that can further expand this concept. Specifically, I will look to works of interactive fiction and videogames as they are made and played, to determine the opportunities for art, design, and media educators who see the importance of the relationship between videogames and ways of making, teaching and researching digital visual art.

In 2013, an independent game designer named Zoe Quinn released a game called *Depression Quest* (2013) that she created with Patrick Lindsey, who assisted with the writing, and Isaac Schankler who composed the music. The game challenged many of the conventions that are commonly associated with videogames: it was primarily text-based, it lacks a triumphant conclusion, and the theme was serious, dealing with depression and social anxiety (Parkin, 2014). It was received with mixed reviews. Many thought that the game was unsuccessful, based upon the qualities listed above, earning it a score of 1.5 out of 10 on the rating website Metacritic. However, others felt that the game shed light on an important social topic indicated by the title (Owen, 2013).

Depression Quest (2013) was certainly not the first video game to deal with serious social issues, or to challenge the conventions of interactivity and narrative. It is described by the creators as being an interactive fiction game. Interactive Fiction games are typically text-based, and they incorporate branching narratives of the type found in choose your own adventure books (IFTF, n.d.). Interactive Fiction games combine features from video games and literature, creating a unique hybrid. *Depression Quest* (2013) can also be understood as a Serious Game. The Serious Games movement that started in the early 2000's looked to applications of video games within areas such as education, advertising, cultural heritage, and health care (Laamarti et al., 2014). These games were designed for a variety of audiences and to be used in numerous ways. What makes them serious games is that the primary purpose is not enjoyment or entertainment. Serious games are typically used to train the player to complete certain tasks or to teach them about various subjects that are deemed culturally relevant.

The aspects of *Depression Quest* (2013) that are related to Interactive Fiction or Serious Games are perhaps not the reason that many are aware of it. Although the game was somewhat controversial when it was released, it was not until an ex-boyfriend of Quinn's named Eron Gjoni accused her of cheating on him with game industry professionals in order to advance her career (VanDerWerff, 2014). This single blog post was quickly shared, and Quinn soon became the focus of a great deal of hatred, to the point where she left that her life was in danger. When her personal details were shared online, she was forced to move out of her apartment and live with a friend. The hashtag #gamergate, which was initially used by those who were incensed by Quinn's alleged wrongdoings, became the locus for intense arguments regarding gender representation and ethics in gaming communities worldwide.

Gamergate has brought longstanding issues of harassment of women in gaming communities to the attention of a larger public. The hatred that was initially directed at Quinn soon spread to individuals, primarily women, who spoke out support of her. Feminist media critic Anita Sarkeesian was the target of death and rape threats that became so troubling that she was forced to cancel public speaking engagements and move from her home, much like Quinn. As Romano (2020) argues, Gamergate has shown the extent to which virulent online harassment and hatred is present, manifested through what is often called "revenge porn," and aided by social media platforms that have failed to police hate speech. These issues extend beyond gaming communities, having been amplified through the mobilization of alt-right and white supremacist groups both online and off.

Interactivity is the fourth aspect of digital visuality. This concept can help art educators, designers, and theorists to better understand the controversial collisions between social issues and cultural forms of expression that have proliferated as video games have become central to contemporary digital visual culture. As discussed in Chapter One, the relationship between interactivity and digital media has been well theorized. While many have found theories of interactivity to be useful in helping to understand the unique qualities of digital media, and digital visual art (Kwastek, 2015), others see in the term much that has yet to be defined and understood. The "myth of interactivity" (Manovich, 2001) is a relevant reference point here, as digital games such as *Cow Clicker* (Bogost, 2010) operate as videogames, but such games frustrate or subvert the ability for interaction to take place on a level that fits within the liberatory rhetoric of videogame studies.

Depression Quest (2013) is an Interactive Fiction game that was created by Zoe Quinn, Patrick Lindsey, and Isaac Schankler in 2013. This game uses the trope of interactivity to raise issues about depression; the player is provided with fewer and fewer choices in an attempt to simulate the immobilizing effects of depression. The game is web-based, which means that you can play it from your web browser,[1] and it is designed so that the title screen is constantly shown on the left-hand side of the screen. Above the title, there is a stack of Polaroid photographs, which appear to be blank. Under the title, it states that the game is an: "interactive (non)fiction about living with depression (n.p.)."

The game begins with a title screen that describes the motivations of the game developers and emphasizes that the aim of the game is to teach the player about depression. There are links to a suicide prevention hotline, and another to allow the player to donate to The National Suicide Prevention Hotline. When you click on the "Begin" button, your screen changes. There is an image of three Polaroid-style photographs at the top of the page. The top photograph depicts an image of a window with bright sunshine streaming through. Below this image is a few paragraphs of text that begin to describe your life:

> You are a mid-twenties human being. You have a significant other named Alex who you are rather fond of, that you have been seeing exclusively for the past few months. The rest of your social circle consists of a variety of friends and acquaintances, some of whom you met at your day job which is a little boring, but pays the rent. You'd like to be doing more with your life, as would your parents, but you're still in the process of figuring out what that means and how to go about it (n.p.).

There are links in this paragraph that begin the branching narrative that continues throughout the game. When you click on the link for "day job" for example, your screen changes. Now the photographs at the top show a close-up of an illuminated computer keyboard. The text describes your day job, which is generally unfulfilling.

In an interactive fiction game, the player is generally provided with a number of choices that guide the narrative of the game. These choices allow the player to internalize aspects of the main character or protagonist. While all fiction enables this, to some degree, it has been argued that the process of choosing for the characters in the digital game strengthens these connections (Robson & Meskin, 2016). What makes *Depression Quest* (2013) unique is that, as the game proceeds, you are provided with numerous choices, but some of these have been written in a red typeface and have been crossed out. The branching choices that are enabled through videogames in general, and interactive fiction games specifically, often take the form of an unfolding narrative or grand quest. The reference to a quest in the title makes this connection clear, but this reference is shaded with irony. Quests in videogames and fantasy literature are usually epic in nature, with the protagonist solving puzzles and vanquishing foes as they discover life-altering things about themselves and the world around them. In *Depression Quest* (2013), this epic journey is not to be found. What unfolds in this quest is a life that becomes more puzzling, foes that become more deadly, and an eventual descent into an immobilizing existence.

The relationship between interactive fiction, videogames, and play can shed light upon the concepts of interconnectness and reflexivity, indeterminacy and variability, and intersectionality and power as related to works of digital art in a Digital Visual Art Education. Digital games have been interconnected since the early days of the internet. With advancements in processing speeds and the cultural acceptance of online forms of interaction came the development of Massively Multiplayer Online Games, or MMO's (Delwiche, 2006). MMO's draw upon the same dynamic interactive connections that help to make the internet the robust space for social interaction. As Delwiche (2006) states:

> These social spaces encourage information sharing and collaboration both within and beyond game parameters. In external message boards, fans discuss strategies, recommend improvements to game software, and share chunks of software code ("mods") that transform rules and content. The distributed learning evident in such forums is

> similar to that found in other knowledge communities, from discussion forums dedicated to sewing to mailing lists focused on programming techniques (n.p.).

Depression Quest (2013) is inherently interconnected as it is presented online. However, the opportunities for interaction with other players made possible by online games is frustrated in this particular game. Though this might be a coincidence, one should see it as an intentional aspect of the game. Depression is inherently isolating, and the inability for one to reach out to other online players as one would in other videogames, for assistance in completing a level or just social interaction, are not coded into gameplay. Researchers looking at the relationship between social media and depression in teenagers have found a dramatic rise in reported depression that correlates with the widespread use of social media sites such as Facebook (Richtel, 2022).

Videogame researchers have struggled to determine the impact of videogames on player identity for some time, and these questions have become more complicated as games have evolved and notions of extrinsic and extrinsic motivations have become more complex (Przybylski et al., 2012). In *Depression Quest* (2013), the identity of the player seems to be a major theme. The player of the game should reflect upon the emotional state of the protagonist and use these reflections to learn about depression and ways to find help when one is depressed. As it states on the homepage for the game:

> The goal of this game is twofold: firstly, we want to illustrate as clearly as possible what depression is like, so that it may be better understood by people without depression. Hopefully this can be something to spread awareness and fight against the social stigma and misunderstandings that depression sufferers face. Secondly, our hope is that in presenting as real a simulation of depression as possible, other sufferers will come to know that they aren't alone, and hopefully derive some measure of comfort from that (n.p.).

Videogames are inherently variable experiences. No two experiences with videogames are ever identical. In fact, most narrative-based videogames make it impossible to ever have the same exact experience due to the unfolding of narrative elements and the winnowing of options that evolve from gameplay. While early videogames offered limited variability, many contemporary videogame experiences present almost-unlimited options for gameplay. As Juul (2007) states:

> Learning to play any game is a process of creating strategies for playing that game, but changing the level layout forces the player to constantly reconsider his or her

> strategies. In the history of video games, this way of creating variation was superseded by data storage, by new games with vast expanses for the player to explore (109).

While this variability may add an element of challenge to the gameplay, and also build in a desire to repeat the gaming experience numerous times, they can also result in feelings of loss that are very real (Krishna, 2021). In *Depression Quest* (2013), the choices made by the player seem to result in less options, indicated by those that are crossed out in red. In this manner, *Depression Quest* (2013) gradually limits the variability experienced by the player, much like depression limits the individual in life.

Intersectional power emphasizes the ways that differing power relationships interact or conflict with one another. Intersectionality as it relates to digital games is directly related to the ways that these experiences are interconnected. Digital visual identity is reflected in the wide variety of digital games that are played around the globe. These experiences are intersectional, as they offer opportunities to reflect upon aspects of individuality, race, class, and gender. These markers of identity are always relational, always tied to one another in a complicated manner. As previously discussed, intersectionality relates to and in many ways runs parallel with the dynamic qualities of decentralized networks as they relate to digital visual works of art. The intersectional aspects of Raimundi's and Musson's work discussed in the previous chapter can be seen in the connections that they make visible. Through their performance-based works that address issues of race, class, and gender, they decenter individual positions of artistic authority. Their identities are continually shifting, marked through the use of a variety of names, and modes of visual self-presentation.

These modes of decentralized identification are enabled in interactive fiction and videogames, to varying degrees and with a number of different effects. Gee (2008) discusses the relationship between videogames and identity as such:

> Video games are all about identity. The player 'plays' some character; the player takes on, carries out, and identifies with some special identity in a virtual world. When I have married my personal goals and values to the virtual character's 'in-game' goals, I see the game as both a project that the game designers have given to me and, simultaneously, I project my own goals, desires, values, and identity into the game world, melded with the 'in-game' identity and goals of the virtual character. The 'project' now becomes 'mine' and not just something imposed on me, because I have 'projected' myself into it (p. 207).

Gee (2008) contends that the player of the videogame is continually shifting between these identities. In the process of toggling between the identity of the player and the identity of the character in the game, a third identity is created. He describes this identity and its relationship to learning thusly:

> Learning involves taking on and playing with identities in such a way that the learner has real choices (in developing the virtual identity) and ample opportunity to meditate on the relationship between new identities and old ones. There is a tripartite play of identities as learners relate, and reflect on, their multiple real-world identities, a virtual identity, and a projective identity.

Gee is describing a form of empathy here. Empathy in videogame play is a contested topic. As previously stated, Quinn and her collaborators intended for the player to feel empathy for the protagonist in *Depression Quest* (2013). However, some videogame theorists are critical of the potential these experiences to build empathy in the player. Ruberg (2020) outlines one such critical position as follows:

> Understanding video games, and especially games by and about marginalized people, through a focus on 'empathy' establishes and justifies discriminatory beliefs about how video game should make players feel and who has the right to experience those feelings (p. 14).

Ruberg is arguing that marginalized people in particular are exploited by videogames that all the player to "walk in their shoes." Though they offer differing interpretations, the potential for videogames to generate empathy is affirmed by both Gee and Ruberg. The primary difference here is how they describe the ways that empathy is leveraged, and who gains from the process of playing videogames in and through a variety of identities.

Contemporary Interactive Fiction games and videogames facilitate intersectional engagements with forms of identity that speak to empathy and agency. Many contemporary digital visual artists draw from and influence videogames, creating intriguing cross-pollination of ideas and visual forms. These digital visual works of art challenge previous notions of interactivity and passivity, instantiations of space, as well as divisions between commercial media and fine art. They also reframe conceptualizations of play that have been reinforced in numerous cultures and across time.

The work of digital visual artists Wafaa Bilal and Yael Kanarek build upon technical, physical, and phenomenological aspects of videogame play, while engaging with traditional modes of artistic production and presentation.

Although generally accepted within the systems of gallery display and globalized art festivals, the presentation and reception of these projects is often confused, and occasionally misleading, in many ways paralleling the challenges of exhibiting early video art. Existing at the intersections of video art and interactive design, between the nodes of art, science, and technology, contemporary videogame play exemplifies the challenges inherent in cross-disciplinary forms of artistic production.

Wafaa Bilal is an Iraqi-born, New York based artist who has used a variety of technologies to reflect upon and critically respond to the Iraq War. In *Virtual Jihadi* (2008), Bilal presented a videogame in which he was the main character, a suicide bomber who is out to avenge his brother's death by hunting down and killing George W. Bush (Bilal, 2008). *Virtual Jihadi* (2008) combines and amplifies the sensationalized aspects of first-person shooters with the political nature of contemporary art. The work is a unique hybrid of both, resting uneasily between the two worlds. When the exhibition of *Virtual Jihadi* (2008) at Rensellaer Polytechnic Institute was cancelled in the Spring of 2009, it brought much of this unease to the surface.

Yael Kanarek is a New York-based artist who works primarily in and through digital environments. Her multifaceted project *World of Awe* (1995–present) is a sprawling travelogue that documents the movements of a traveler through space and time, using the interface of the traveler's laptop as portal. The first chapter of *World of Awe* (1995–present) was featured in the 2002 Whitney Biennial, along with renderings of some of the reference images from the work. As the opening page states:

> Salvaged off a laptop, World of Awe 1.0 contains the journal of a traveler in search of a lost treasure. Navigate through personal love letters, log entries and detailed technical descriptions of the unusual navigation tools. Special efforts were made to maintain the authenticity of this collection by mirroring its original format (n.p.).

Though not a direct reference to contemporary videogames, *World of Awe* (1995–present) does share many similarities with early computer-based role-playing games such as *Oregon Trail* (1971), and with Interactive Fiction games such as *Depression Quest* (2013). With a multilayered series of narratives and images, World of Awe offers the viewer numerous points of entry, romanticizing previous graphical user interfaces and remediating the travelogue for the postdigital age.

Both of these artists incorporate and respond to aspects of contemporary videogame play; each has, in turn, encountered challenges when attempting to exhibit work in traditional venues. In many ways, the institutional confusion created runs parallel to the challenges faced by early video artists in the 1970's. Early video art represented the collision between a popular medium and a range of practices deemed above such commercial concerns. Video was seen as a radical form of production that could unsettle the hierarchies that had dominated the artworld for decades, if not centuries:

> Many artists in the early days of video art believed that video, especially two-way video in which viewers might also be producers, had the potential to decentralise television and wrest control of content from corporate commercial programming and its one way broadcasting model of distribution and consumption (Wood, 2009, 187).

In many cases, video was incorporated into the existing gallery structure in a seamless, uncritical manner. Typically, video art was simply displayed on a monitor, prompting a mode of viewership that had been inculcated through years of television watching (Caldwell, 1995). A few artists, such as Nam June Paik, started to interrogate the space of the gallery through installation-based video work, forming a thread of inquiry that was not taken up by the majority of video artists and curators at the time.

It is conjecture at this point to argue that video art was successful or unsuccessful in changing the gallery system, or the options available for television viewers. What is interesting to consider is the current parallel between video art and the artworld and interactive media, in the forms described earlier. The rise of social media in the early 2000's and the labeling of Web 2.0 were social shifts that were described as open, democratic, and participatory. (Jenkins, 2006). Videogames make up a large portion of this media landscape; art, design, and media educators who wish to address the unique qualities of videogame play in a Digital Visual Art Education would be well served by studying the successes and failures of video art.

One such example would be *Shoot* (1971), by Chris Burden. In this infamous piece of performance art, Burden is shot in the arm at close range with a. 22 rifle. The piece was attended by a small group of viewers and was documented in black and white photographs and a 15 second video. (Schjeldahl, 2007) Though most would not call Burden a video artist, his work nonetheless relies upon video as documentation. Burden has historically tended to limit the documentation of his work, releasing only grainy footage that furthers the obscure nature of the work:

> By acknowledging the real distance between the live event and the secondary audience, instead of trying to compensate for it, Burden's documentation conveys a hype-free authenticity even as it tends to mythify the work by omitting distracting details (Horvitz, 1974)

Comparing this work to *Domestic Tension* (2005) by Waafa Bilal, we can see a shift in the role that the media plays in the reception of both pieces. In *Domestic Tension* (2005), we see Bilal on a webcam in a nondescript room, furnished with a couch, a desk, a desktop computer, and a paintball gun mounted on a table. As described by Bilal:

> During the course of the exhibition, Bilal will confine himself to the gallery space. Over the duration, people will have 24-hour virtual access to the space via the Internet. They will have the ability to watch Bilal and interact with him through a live web-cam and chat room. Should they choose to do so, viewers will also have the option to shoot Bilal with a paintball gun, transforming the virtual experience into a very physical one (Bilal, 2005, n.p.)

Where Burden is shot by a. 22 rifle, Bilal is shot by paintballs operated from a distance, by participants logging in to a related website. Burden's work was instantly mythologized due to its limited viewership, while Bilal's work is all distanced viewership: a webcam captures images of him being shot, and a blog documents his experiences. Bilal has discussed this piece in relationship to the remote warfare being waged in Iraq and Afghanistan. It resonates on a individualistic level, as Bilal's brother was killed in 2003 as a result of a US drone strike. This clearly leads to an acknowledgement of race and ethnicity. How often are contemporary videogame players provided with the opportunity to commit acts of violence towards people of color who are framed as "terrorists" through language emanating from the US Global War on Terror? What socioeconomic class are the targets of such violence. And how does gender relate to these digital acts of violence?

Each of these questions can be explored through an analysis of the work of Bilal as it relates to the concepts of interactivity and play. Descriptions of interactivity can be applied to digital visual works of art so that contemporary relationships between viewer and artwork can be better understood. In the case of videogame play, there is much to be learned from how technologies are manipulated, identities are constituted and reconstituted, and how these processes relate to power as it exists in sociocultural contexts. In *World of Awe* (1995–present), the player is not placed into a specific role. Information on race, class or gender is not provided. This results in a reliance upon a default character which one might assume is white, male, and upper class, based upon Western sociotechnical biases.

The only prompt given is that the files of a traveler have been made available, and that they might be of interest to you. You are therefore part detective, part voyeur, and part explorer. As stated on the Rhizome Net Art Anthology website (2016):

> Chapter 1 brings a new cultural interface—the computer desktop—to a timeless narrative genre, the travelogue, and to the enduring artists' task of worldbuilding. In doing so, it evokes the ever-present longing, isolation, and ruin that are the repressed remainders of digital culture.

Reading the journal of the traveler allows the player access to the internal thoughts and motivations of this character. In this manner, the player has the opportunity to play as the traveler character, to compare these experiences with their own, and potentially create the tripartite identity formation theorized by Gee (2008).

In *Domestic Tension* (2005), the player identity is also drawn into a relationship with the character on the screen, who happens to be Bilal himself. The artwork draws out issues related to wars in distant lands that are increasingly fought using remote weapons of war. As Bilal (2005) describes:

> Bilal's self imposed confinement is designed to raise awareness about the life of the Iraqi people and the home confinement they face due to the both the violent and the virtual war they face on a daily basis. This sensational approach to the war is meant to engage people who may not be willing to engage in political dialogue through conventional means. Domestic Tension will depict the suffering of war not through human displays of dramatic emotion, but rather through engaging people in the sort of playful interactive video game with which they are familiar (n.p.).

This interactive play is critical to the ways that the viewer/player interacts with both digital visual works discussed in this section. The folder and file system that was used in early personal computing systems is clearly referenced in *World of Awe* (1995–present), which establishes a historical reference point while it also uses a familiar interface for the user. However, these desktop file systems are generally not played with, as one would play a videogame, for example. This introduces an element of unfamiliarity to the experience, just as the references to first-person play in *Domestic Tension* (2005) are reframed through the very real shooting taking place.

Interactive forms of play as discussed through the examples of digital video art and digital games can allow for issues of agency and identity to be foregrounded. In a Digital Visual Art Education, these concepts are critical, as they expand beyond applications of digital media that are purely technical and formal. Opportunities for art educators to engage with these concepts, along with the implications for interconnected reflexivity and indeterminate variability, will now be discussed in the concluding chapter.

Notes

1 The gameplay that is described took place in late 2020, during the writing of this chapter. Many aspects of the game may have changed since it was first released, which is common in both web-based and console-based videogames.

References

Bogost, I. (2011). The End of Gamers. In *How to Do Things With Videogames* (pp. 147–154). University of Minnesota Press. http://www.jstor.org/stable/10.5749/j.cttttmwd.24

Businessweek. (2020). *Global Mobile Gaming Market Report 2020: Worth $98 Billion in 2020, the Mobile Gaming Market Is Forecast to Grow to $272 Billion by 2030*. Accessed June, 23, from https://www.businesswire.com/news/home/20210625005180/en/Global-Mobile-Gaming-Market-Report-202-Worth-98-Billion-in-2020-the-Mobile-Gaming-Market-is-Forecast-to-Grow-to-272-Billion-by-2030---ResearchAndMarkets.com

Delwiche, A. (2006). Massively Multiplayer Online Games (MMOs) in the New Media Classroom. *Educational Technology and Society*, 9(3), 160–172.

Galloway, A. (2006). *Gaming: Essays on Algorithmic Culture*. University of Minnesota Press.

Gee, J. P. (2007). *What Video Games Have to Teach Us About Learning and Literacy* (2nd ed.). St. Martins Griffin.

Gee, J. P. (2008). Learning Theory, Video Games, and Popular Culture. In K. Drotner & S. Livingstone (Eds.), *The International Handbook of Children, Media and Culture* (pp. 196–210). Sage.

Interactive Fiction Technology Foundation. (n.d.). *Frequently Asked Questions About Interactive Fiction*. Accessed from https://iftechfoundation.org/frequently-asked-questions/

Juul, J. (2007). Variation Over Time: The Transformation of Space in Single-Screen Action Games. In F. Borries, S. Walz, U. Brinkmann, & M. Böttger (Eds.), *Space Time Play* (pp. 100–109). Birkhäuser.

Konzack, L. (2007). Rhetorics of Computer and Video Game Research. In J. P. Williams & J. H. Smith (Eds.), *'The Players' Realm: Studies on the Culture of Video Games and Gaming*. London: McFarland and Company, Inc.

Krishna, S. (2021). The Real Pleasure and Pain of Making Choices in Video Games. *Wired*. Accessed May, 2022, from https://www.wired.com/story/casual-gamer-video-game-decisions/

Laamarti, F., Eid, M., & El Saddik, A. (2014). An Overview of Serious Games. *International Journal of Computer Games Technology*. https://doi.org/10.1155/2014/358152

Lupton, C., & Mcdonald, P. (2010). Reflexivity as Entertainment: Early Novels and Recent Video Games. *Mosaic: An Interdisciplinary Critical Journal*, *43*(4), 157–173. http://www.jstor.org/stable/44030298

Manovich, L. (2001). *The Language of New Media*. MIT Press.

Markey, P., & Ferguson, C. (2017). Teaching Us to Fear: The Violent Video Game Moral Panic and the Politics of Game Research. *American Journal of Play*, *10*(1), 99–115.

Owen, P. (2013). *4 Videogames that Help You Understand and Deal with Your Depression*. Kotaku.

Parkin, S. (2014). Zoe Quinn's Depression Quest (2013). *The New Yorker*. Accessed from https://www.newyorker.com/tech/annals-of-technology/zoe-quinns-depression-quest

Patton, R. M. (2013). Games as an Artistic Medium: Investigating Complexity Thinking in Game-Based Art Pedagogy. *Studies in Art Education*, *55*(1), 35–50. http://www.jstor.org/stable/24465508

Przybylski, A. K., Weinstein, N., Murayama, K., Lynch, M. F., & Ryan, R. M. (2012). The Ideal Self at Play: The Appeal of Video Games That Let You Be All You Can Be. *Psychological Science*, *23*(1), 69–76. http://www.jstor.org/stable/41416995

Richtel, M. (2022). 'It's Life or Death': The Mental Health Crisis Among U.S. Teens. *The New York Times*. Accessed May 11, 2022, from https://www.nytimes.com/2022/04/23/health/mental-health-crisis-teens.html

Robson, J., & Meskin, A. (2016). Video Games as Self-Involving Interactive Fictions. *The Journal of Aesthetics and Art Criticism*, *74*(2), 165–177. http://www.jstor.org/stable/44510494

Romano, A. (2020). *What We Still Haven't Learned from Gamergate*. Vox. Accessed fromhttps://www.vox.com/2014/9/6/6111065/gamergate-explained-everybody-fighting

Ruberg, B. (2020). Empathy and Its Alternatives: Deconstructing the Rhetoric of "Empathy" in Video Games. *Communication, Culture & Critique*, 1–18. Oxford University Press on behalf of International Communication Association.

Squire, K. (2006). From Content to Context: Videogames as Designed Experience. *Educational Researcher*, *35*(8), 19–29. http://www.jstor.org/stable/4124789

VanDerWerff, E. (2014). *#Gamergate: Here's Why Everybody in the Video Game World Is Fighting*. Vox. Accessed from https://www.vox.com/2014/9/6/6111065/gamergate-explained-everybody-fighting

· 6 ·

DIGITAL VISUAL ART EDUCATION

In this final chapter, I will summarize the main points that I have made throughout this book. Following this summary, I will provide an overview of how these points might be utilized in art, design, and media education. In Chapter One, I outlined the basic concept of digital visuality. Digital visuality will be discussed in this chapter as it relates to artmaking, teaching, and research, with the goal that these areas help to contribute to the set of approaches that I am calling Digital Visual Art Education. To speak to these dynamic qualities of vision and visuality, we must take into consideration how these qualities are foregrounded in previous artistic research and practice. Once these are discussed, the potential for future approaches for art and design-based research and practices that acknowledges the relevance of digital visuality within a Digital Visual Art Education will be offered.

Before I engage in this line of thinking, I will reiterate two ways that digital visuality can be understood. The first way is when visuality is questioned and supplanted in digital visual works of art. Here the central role that visuality plays in digital visual works of art is drawn into question. This can be seen in *Eyes* (2018), by Yoon Chung Han. In this digital visual work of art the eye is made into data, sculptural form, and sound. It can be seen in the work of *Tracking Transience* (2003–present), by Hasan Elahi, where the photographic record of his daily life overwhelms the viewer, becoming perhaps more easily seen as data. The second way that digital visuality can be understood is through digital visual works of art that present visuality as fragmented, multiplied, and fractured. Here the centrality of a fixed image is challenged through multiple images that complete with one another. In *Tracking Transience* (2003–present), there is no one viewpoint that the viewer can use to assess the work, due to its presentation and massive amount of data. It is only able to be viewed in fragments. It is also variable, in that it is presented online, and in numerous gallery and museum exhibitions. In *Eyes* (2018), the work is made from multiple components, including the eye of the viewer, the camera that captures the image of the eye, the computer program that makes the data from the image, the screen that presents the data visualization of the eye, the program that translates the data into sound, the audio system that reproduces the sound, and the 3D printer that makes a sculptural form from the data files.

The first form of digital visuality should be thought of as being primarily theoretical, and is related to the content of the work, the intent of the artist, and the interpretation of the viewer. The second form of digital visuality should be thought of as being primarily structural, and is related to the form of the work, and the mode of presentation. Both are interrelated, but because they are based upon the traditional split between form and content that is found in Western art theory, they can also be applied individually. Art educators have structured a great deal of their approaches towards teaching and understanding art according to the form/content dyad. Art educators such as Sandell (2009) have expanded this binary to include context, but in this case the initial structure is not questioned; it is added to. Artists, educators, and researchers who are engaged with digital visual works of art should consider expanding these relationships and critiquing existing binaries as they study digital media that are currently emerging.

Digital Visual Art Education and Digital Visuality

As I have discussed, a Digital Visual Art Education is important for art, design, and media educational researchers who are looking to study, understand, and teach about digital visual works of art. The concept of visuality should be thought of as the sociocultural influences that impact how we see what we see, and as such it includes but extends beyond the visual arts. As Bryson (1988) states: "Between retina and world is inserted a screen of signs, a screen consisting of all the multiple discourses on vision built into the social arena." These multiple discourses are essential for art educational researchers to acknowledge, specifically as they are multiplied, fragmented, and expanded through networked digital technologies. Visuality has been discussed by numerous art, design, and media educators, introduced by works such as John Berger's (1970) Ways of Seeing. The sociocultural aspects of vision and the power relationships that undergird these aspects were described in detail by theorists in the Frankfurt School; it was specifically Walter Benjamin who spoke to the use of visuality by German Fascists before World War II, which influenced Berger directly.

Discussions of visuality likely gained traction as art theorists started to look to visual culture as a set of theories relevant for art educational practices in the late 1990's. In his essay "What is Visual Culture," Mirzoeff (1998) states the following: "Visual culture does not depend upon pictures but on this modern tendency to picture or visualize existence" (p. 6). This conceptualization of visual culture allowed many art educators to extend their practices beyond formal readings of works of art and expand their frame of reference to include works from popular culture (Freedman, 2003). For example, Walker (2004) analyzes contemporary works of art through theories of visuality to explore possibilities for art educational pedagogy, while Emme (2001) discusses the activist potential of visuality as art educational research.

In these examples, visuality is presented as a concept that art educators can speak to from a unique perspective, and that can be leveraged in both teaching and research. Looking at visuality from a conceptual perspective, Garoian (2010) writes about the subversive potential to be found in what he terms *prosthetic visuality*. For Garoian, visual art can function as a prosthetic that allows for the disruption of previous modes of visuality and representation. In a related manner that is more specific to digital technologies, Tervo (2012) suggests a visuality based in digital dysfunction that extends beyond visual representation in his analysis of the work of jan jagodzinski:

> I claim that the self-refleXive events that jagodzinski argued for can be found outside the realm of contemporary art, where the ephemerality and vulnerability of digital data (not objects, following jagodzinski's critique) is very prevalent. Although this data can be easily captured by the neoliberal economy, we should not preclude ourselves to examine their possibilities of revealing gaps in the Symbolic-Imaginary economy of signs. For example, as one's image in Skype pixellates into nebulous blur

> or as a video stream that emanates gleaming carnal lust stops due to the failure to connect to the server, the magic of screen culture disappears, leaving the subject alone with its own insatiable desires and failed representation. This is, I claim, a form of visuality that needs more theorizing among art educators and, most importantly, more attention as a strategy that allows us to go beyond representation. (p. 83)

Here we can see an argument for the acknowledgement of the dysfunctional aspects of digital media that is similar to what I have theorized previously. Where Tervo (2012) describes the potential for digital data to reveal gaps in the Symbolic Imaginary, based in the theories of Lacan, I have argued that dysfunctional digital technologies disrupt utopian conceptualizations of digital technologies (See Sweeny, 2015). Digital visuality takes into account this dysfunction, looking to moments of failure as enabling constraints. Artists, educators, and theorists who are researching digital works of art should consider the ways that such artists leverage the dysfunctional aspects of vision; the limits of what can be seen, as well as the ways that such limits might point to new forms of visuality and visibility. Visibility here relates to the relationship between the tools used to make the digital work of art, and the work of art as presented to the viewer. This is a relationship that is familiar to many artists, educators, and theorists, as it relates closely to the form/content dichotomy that underlies many traditional concepts of making in Western studio art traditions.

Freedman (2003) describes how digital technologies might impact these traditions as they relate to visual culture:

> A critical debate in the arts and education concerns the place of visual forms produced through the use of the computer and other advanced technologies. The debate is also about the dissemination of visual culture, including traditional art forms, through the use of these technologies. Computer technology is not only a medium—it is a means—and it is largely experienced as visual. It has enabled people to see things previously unimagined, to cross borders of traditional form in the fine arts, to the mass media, and to scientific visualization. (p. 16)

While I might take issue with the notion that these experiences are "largely experienced as visual," I would certainly agree that computer technologies should be viewed as both medium and means by art educators. Art educators who attempt to use digital media in their practices are often challenged by the notion that the computer is only a tool. Contemporary digital media have expanded beyond the beige box in the corner of the classroom, museum, or studio. Digital media are embedded and embodied, and as such offer art educators numerous possibilities to channel the power of the technologies, while at the same time critiquing this very power.

Along these lines, there have been art educators such as Knochel and Patton (2015) who have argued that teaching art students to code can provide them with a powerful way to both make and understand the ways that digital media are made. A Digital Visual Art Education must acknowledge the aspects of digital visual art that are visible, as well as those that operate below the surface of visibility. Digital visual artists such as Yoon and Elahi can provide art educational researchers with relevant examples of digital visuality that can be addressed by strategies that come out of a Digital Visual Art Education-based approach to making, teaching, and researching.

Reflexivity

The first aspect of digital visuality that artists, educators, and researchers should acknowledge is the decentralized reflexivity that relates to digital works of art. As I have discussed, the ability for digital visual works of art to use visuality in order to reflect upon visuality should be thought of as a feedback loop. In electronic communications, these feedback loops help to optimize the ways that networks can transmit messages. In digital visual works of art, these reflexive feedback loops can optimize the flows of information as they relate to the communication of a theme or message. They can also present the viewer with a message that is unclear, where noise is incorporated in the message, or the message fails to send altogether. This is the dysfunctional aspect of networked digital technologies that I argue art educators can learn much from.

I have written extensively on the topic of feedback loops as they relate to art educational practices. In art educational scholarship, however, there has not been much acknowledgement of feedback of this type. One notable exception can be found in Wilson and Wilson (1977), where they describe the process of drawing through the extended metaphor of the *drawing-an-object program*:

> As far as a program for drawing is concerned, one could think of the mind as a programmer for the computer/brain… The programmer dimension of mind is the source of signals containing generalized notions regarding the way in which drawings ought to look. When a signal is sent from the programmer to the computer brain that a particular object is to be drawn, a hierarchically ordered set of functions is set into

> motion. As the hand-held tool begins to mark on a surface, the sensory receptor experiences a flow of energy or intensity as well as sensation or the quality of intensity. The configuration (of the object to be drawn) is remembered (p. 7).

Here we can see a cybernetic description of the drawing process. Cybernetic concepts were fashionable at the time in which this was written. What is most relevant for the discussion of reflexive feedback loops here is the way that Wilson and Wilson (1977) describe difficulties in the process:

> During the running of the drawing-an-object program, a comparator notes discrepancies between the delineated forms and the remembered configuration. Error signals trigger corrective action through changes in transitions and sequences until the delineation comes into close enough correspondence to the remembered configuration that troublesome errors are no longer signalled and the drawing of an object is considered complete. The other possibility is that the errors signalled are of such magnitude as to cause the entire program to be aborted, to be replayed or, in rare cases, never to be attempted again (p. 7).

The feedback described here is related to the interaction between sight and touch, between the concept of the drawing and the drawing produced through the process. The computer program is used here as a metaphor. An example that speaks to feedback loops that are specific to contemporary digital technologies can be found in May (2011). Here, May argues for a decentralized approach to conceiving of art curricula, taking advantage of the flexibility and the participatory qualities found in decentralized networks.

Decentralized reflexivity must be seen as an important element in the study of digital visual works of art, in both the process of making as described by Wilson and Wilson (1977) and in the creation of curricula (May, 2011). This reflexivity is highlighted in works such as *Eyes* (2018) and *Tracking Transience* (2003–present); in both, the way that we look is folded back into the work itself, allowing us to critically assess the role that vision plays in a digital visual culture. Both works also share the tools that are used to make the works, allowing for further derivations to be created.

Variability

The second aspect of digital visuality that digital artists, educators, and researchers should acknowledge is the variability that is shown in digital works of art. As Manovich (2001) argued, variability is an important component of new media works of art, one that allows them to be broken apart and reconfigured in myriad ways, maintaining a level of indeterminacy. This process is directly tied to traditional approaches based in appropriation, and in more contemporary remix strategies.

The use of the remix as academic metaphor does not occur until the early 2000's; prior to this time, there are writings about the remix in music and poetry, but these tend to present remix as an artistic approach. In art educational research, there have been a number of studies that look to the potential of the remix. These studies all originate after the year 2000, as this term rose to prominence in academia in the late 1990's. In his 2009 editorial in *Studies in Art Education*, Blandy describes the potential for the remix as a form of democratic participation. In a similar manner, Duncum (2014) looks to YouTube video production as a relevant site for art educational research and production, which I discussed in Chapter Four.

Friere and McCarthy (2014) explore the possibilities for the remix in art educational lesson planning and pedagogy, identifying possibilities for collaboration while they address issues of copyright and intellectual property. Knochel (2013) addresses how these issues relate to a social media landscape, through work with university undergraduate students: "Assembling visuality using social media allows for the visual culture of crowds to provide a vast array of media input in visual construction that is perhaps a unique resource that distinguishes social media as a visual apparatus" (p. 21). In my own work, I have explored the possibilities for the variability of digital media to tease out similar questions in art educational research, looking specifically at how this quality relates to the concept of networked identity (Sweeny, 2009b).

The variable and indeterminate nature of digital works of art can offer artists, educators, and researchers numerous avenues for exploration and inquiry. They should look specifically at the ways that digital media open possibilities for new forms of visuality while they foreclose upon others. In the case of *Tracking Transience* (2003–present), we see Elahi's daily life in a steady flow of images, which makes the scrutiny of individual images challenging at best. In addition, art educators should pay careful attention to the implications related to media remixing as it is further embedded in digital programs, mobile apps, and social media platforms. The ease with which one can cut, paste, reconfigure, and distribute variable media can lead to an unquestioning relationship with these processes.

Power

The last aspect of digital visuality that art, design, and media educators should acknowledge is the relationship between intersectional forms of power as represented by dataveillance within digital works of art. As I have discussed, there is a meaningful and perhaps troubling connection between networked digital media and mechanisms of observation and control. These connections have only increased as digital devices have become less expensive, more portable, and are marketed as an essential element of a contemporary life.

Art, design, and media educators have the ability to reflect upon this situation, from a unique perspective. As I argued in my research paper "Visual Culture of Control" (2006), the theorization of visual culture in art educational practices needed to seriously consider surveillance as a mode of viewing that shifted the discussion from the viewer to one who is viewed. This situation has only increased in the years since this piece was published, as digital visual culture, and social media specifically has created a platform for the voluntary sharing of personal data.

Though not speaking to dataveillance specifically, Sullivan (2014) discusses the possibilities for data analysis in art educational research practices:

> If we are interested in change that is sustainable, we need to put the ownership of the information in the hands of the user. Data visualization and data mapping is a case in point. These methods are very intuitive approaches to accessing and understanding how data might be relevant to specific situations and settings—one gets to see information in any number of forms and this has high communicative utility. (p. 284)

These are practices that can raise important issues regarding power and visuality with art education students and fellow researchers. They can also speak to the fetishization of data that is a potential outgrowth of digital visual culture. Data fetishization is commonly associated with Big Data, and specifically the Quantified Self (QS) movement (Sharon & Zandbergen, 2016). The work of both Yoon and Elahi identify and isolate different aspects of QS in their work. In *Eyes* (2018), Yoon speaks to the information that can be contained in the human iris, which can stand as a marker for individual identity. In *Tracking Transience* (2003–present), Elahi takes part in an obsessive cataloguing of daily activity, which is one of the hallmarks of QS. Both digital visual artists speak to the use of data to control, but in different ways. Yoon is referencing the control by another, while Elahi is speaking to one controlling oneself.

Data fetishization is also an issue in public education, where students are tracked and monitored with increasing frequency and precision. Art educators can speak to these issues through practices that identify and critique such monitoring, especially when it becomes overbearing. In my theorization of the *Pedagopticon* (2009a) (Figure 6.1), I suggest that art educators embrace these practices wholeheartedly, becoming the all-seeing camera eye in the classroom. This parody has unfortunately become very close to what public school teachers in the US are asked to do on a daily basis. However, the *Pedagopticon* (2009) as theorized is primarily visual; the monitoring that is happening in public schools is now being augmented, and perhaps overtaken by dataveillance. (Lupton & Williamson, 2017).

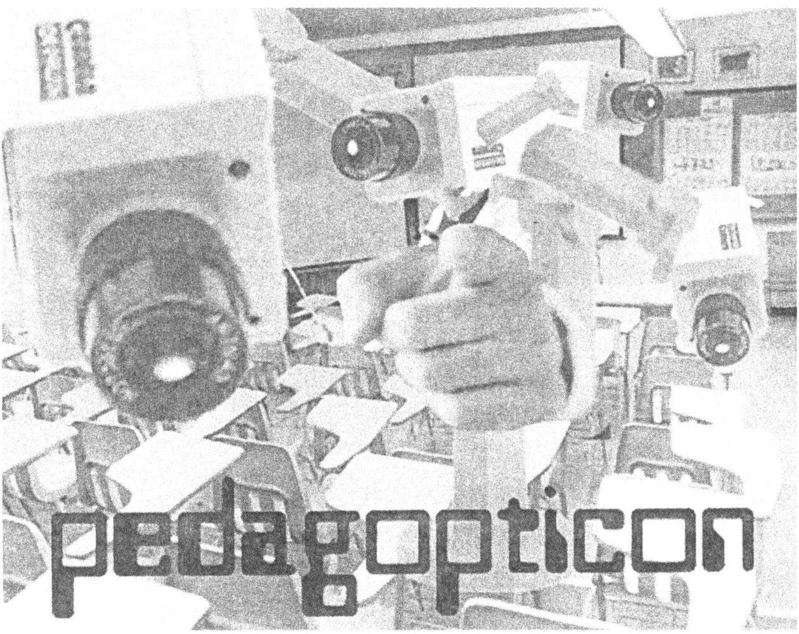

Figure 6.1. Pedagopticon (2009), Robert W. Sweeny

Source: Sweeny, R. (2009a). The Pedagopticon. Other Eyes in the 21st Century Classroom. *Journal for Social Theory in Art Education*. 28. Accessed from https://scholarscompass.vcu.edu/jstae/vol28/iss1/7/. Used with permission of the artist.

Art educational researchers interested in a Digital Visual Art Education should address the aspects of digital visuality that I have identified in this section. Exploring issues of interconnected reflexivity, indeterminate variability, interactive play, and intersectional power will allow for those researchers to adapt their studies as digital technologies continue to proliferate and change over time. These four aspects of Digital Visual Art Education emerge from the four aspects of digital visuality that I have outlined in this book. I will begin my discussion of how these aspects can inform a Digital Visual Art Education with a review of interconnectedness.

Digital Visual Art Education Is Interconnected

The first aspect of digital visuality that art, design, and media educators should acknowledge is the interconnected reflexivity that it relates to digital works of art. The ability for digital visual works of art to use visual means in order to reflect upon visuality should be thought of as a feedback loop. In electronic communications, these feedback loops help to optimize the ways that networks can transmit messages. In digital visual works of art, these reflexive feedback loops can optimize the flows of information as they relate to the communication of a theme or message. They can also present the viewer with a message that is unclear, where noise is incorporated in the message, or the message fails to send altogether.

Interconnected reflexivity must be seen as an important element in the study of digital visual works of art, in both the process of making art as described by Wilson and Wilson (1977) and in the creation of art curricula (May, 2011). This reflexivity is highlighted in digital visual works of art such as *Eyes* (2018) by Yoon Chung Han and *Tracking Transience* (2003–present) by Hasan Elahi. In both works, the way that we look is folded back into the work itself in a feedback loop, allowing us to critically assess the role that vision plays in a Digital Visual Art Education. Both works also share the tools that are used to make the works, allowing for further derivations and related works to be created.

While feedback loops are central to the functioning of complex systems, they are especially important in the modes of interaction that are fostered by social media. These modes of interaction were discussed in Chapter Two through the analysis of internet memes, where meme circulation related to the interconnected reflexivity of digital visuality. Specifically, the process of replicating memes creates both individual memes while it impacts larger groups of memes that are related. Data visualization was also discussed in this chapter as related to a Digital Visual Art Education. Data visualization is inherently interconnected, as the ability to draw upon large data sets relies upon such interconnections. The reflexivity of data visualization also is reliant upon the data being represented. As discussed in Chapter Three, the ways of making that are related to makerspaces and the maker movement help to create reflexive experiences. The useless machines made by Giertz (2018) each speak to needs that she has identified in her daily life. But because the machines are dysfunctional, these needs are never satisfied. The utopian promises offered by technologies are inevitably shown to be out of reach or destined for failure.

Digital visual artists using contemporary social media platforms such as YouTube participate in these reflexive processes as discussed in Chapter Four. Digital visual artists Wanda Raimundi and Jason Musson create alternative identities that reflect upon aspects of race, class, and gender. What happens in the process of the Raimundi and Musson performances is that their specific use of language points to the gaps between speaker and viewer. As I propose, the model of the decentralized network theorized by Baran (1964) allows art, design, and media educators to acknowledge these moments of disruption, and to fold them into educational practice in a reflexive manner.

Digital Visual Art Education is Indeterminate

The second component of digital visuality is indeterminacy. In indeterminacy, the structural and functional aspects of digital visual works of art are brought to the fore. The variable and indeterminate nature of digital works of art can offer art, design, and media educators numerous avenues for exploration and inquiry. In Chapter One I discussed *Tracking Transience* (2003–present), by Hasan Elahi. This digital visual work of art presents a challenge to the viewer as it is an ongoing flow of images that makes the scrutiny of individual images challenging at best.

In Chapter Two I discussed social media and the ways that memes relate to indeterminate variability. The work of Yoon (2014) and De la Rosa-Carrillo (2015) point to the challenges of making memes in the space of art, design, and media education. The automated process of meme generation and circulation enters the maker into conversations about originality and uniqueness in potentially intriguing ways. In this chapter the digital visual artwork of Dennis Delgado was discussed within the framework of data visualization. The photographic images featured in *The Dark Database* (2021) are each composed of individual images selected from films by directors of color through algorithmic processes. This type of data visualization is, somewhat ironically, hard to see. This indeterminacy speaks to the subjugated position that people of color have historically had in the Western film industry. And considering that the films that Delgado are all from the 21st century, we can determine that this situation has not improved, even as calls for racial justice are clearly enunciated by movements such as Black Lives Matter.

Digital Visual Art Education is Intersectional

Intersectionality is the third aspect of a digital visuality. Works of digital visual art speak to this concept through experiences that emphasize agency and identity. In Chapter One I focused on the intersectional aspects of power as related to digital visuality. The work of both Yoon Chung Han and Hasan Elahi identify and isolate different aspects of intersectional power. In *Eyes* (2018), Yoon speaks to the information that can be contained in the human iris, which can stand as a marker for individual identity. In *Tracking Transience* (2003–present), Elahi takes part in an obsessive cataloguing of daily activity, which stands as a collective data visualization of identity.

In Chapter Four, I focused on individuality, gender, race, and class in my discussion of digital visual identity. As mentioned, gender is framed in very specific, provocative ways in the YouTube videos of Raimundi and Musson. In art educational research, there have been decades of studies that have looked to the concept of gender as it relates to the making and understanding of art. However, studies that speak to the relationship between gender and digital media in the field are less common. In one example, Liao (2010) discusses her machinima (machine cinema) work with pre-service art education students. As she writes: "They each created a gender-ambiguous avatar in order to challenge the existing gender representation… They made a music video -like machinima out of their performance to express their effort to disrupt stereotypical gendered avatars" (p. 187). Here, Liao is encouraging her students to analyze forms of gender representation of avatars in digital spaces such as Second Life. The freedom of self-representation in networked online environments has been consistently theorized, especially by well-intentioned art educators such as Liao. However, as these environments are derived from existing spaces and modes of interaction, they are just as prone to gender bias, not to mention racism, xenophobia, and many other types of bigotry (Nakamura, 2007).

In Chapter Two, I discussed social media and memes as they relate to intersectional power. The emergence of *Digital Blackface* identified by Abreu (n.d.) represents the colonialist impulse as it is applied to networked digital interactions. This colonialist impulse has only been amplified by platforms such as YouTube, and, more recently, TikTok (Parham, 2020). Similar situations have been identified by art educators concerned with the influence of popular visual culture on art pedagogy (Parks, 2004). In this chapter I also discussed intersectionality as related to data visualization. Data visualization seems a perfect way to assess the intersectional aspects of gender, class, and race, as it makes visible the often-unacknowledged connections between such markers of identity. However, as the work of Dennis Delgado shows, often artists of color are invisible within these intersections. The digital technologies that can help to apprehend large sets of data are also programmed by individuals with biases and prejudices, and these forces certainly influence the ways that data visualizations are formed and understood.

In Chapter Three, the maker movement was presented as it relates to digital visual artists such as Simone Giertz. Here, the intersectional qualities of the maker movement were shown through the related fields of hobbyists and DIY makers, and the interests of business owners and educators. These fields are often at odds with one another, but the opportunities for art, design, and media educators to identify these varying power relationships, and channel them in their own practices, represent a challenge that is unique to our time. I also discussed the challenges that AI-based art and NFT art represent regarding issues of originality and ethics. Both relate closely to the power dynamics that are central to a Digital Visual Art Education.

Digital Visual Art Education is Interactive

Interactivity is the fourth component of digital visuality. The relationship between interactivity and digital play can be discussed through videogames such as *Cow Clicker* (2010) and works of Interactive Fiction such as *Depression Quest* (2015). In *Depression Quest* the game provides numerous opportunities for the player to make choice-based decisions, in a manner that is intended to generate empathy. This form of interactivity runs counter to the descriptions of videogames as yet another moral panic. Supposedly violent videogames are seen as having a negative influence on the player, or, at best are just a waste of time, as jagodzinski (2007) theorizes. The interactive nature of contemporary videogame play is central to the experience as a work of digital visual art.

In Chapter Five I analyzed the relationship between interactivity and digital play. The influence of *Depression Quest* (2015), and the disruptions caused by the related series of Gamergate incidents, were cited as examples that show that contemporary videogames can speak to audiences beyond those in the gaming community. Gamergate specifically demonstrates the work that needs to be done in gaming communities that continue to harbor sexist and racist beliefs. The interactive aspects of contemporary videogames present opportunities for educators to addresses issues related to identity formation such as gender, race, and class.

I also noted the ways that videogames provide the player with experiences that are indeterminate and variable. Interactive works such as *World of Awe* (2005) by Yael Kanarek present both diegetic and extradiegetic experiences that make each experience with the work unique. In a similar manner, *Domestic Tension* (2005) by Wafaa Bilal uses the familiar interface of the first-person shooter to confuse the divide between public and private space and raise ethical questions about videogames and violence.

Now that I have reviewed the components of digital visuality as they have been discussed, I will return to the main themes introduced in each chapter, in order to expand upon these components. These main themes are: Digital Virality and Data Visualization; Post-digital Materiality and Makerspaces; Digital Play and Videogames; and Digital Visual Identity and Digital Video. My goal here is to connect these themes with art, design, and media education research, and to explore possibilities for a Digital Visual Art Education.

Digital Virality and Digital Visual Art Education

Internet memes have been discussed previously as forms of digital visual art that are collectively constructed, and that mutate as they circulate through digital communicational channels. Here I will entertain the idea that such forms of digital virality might be of use to art, design, and media educators who are interested in engaging in explorations of social media as a form of artistic expression.

There have been several art educators who have researched different aspects of social media. Roland (2010) writes about the possibilities for social media and the social web, which was termed Web 2.0. In his paper titled "Preparing Art Teachers to Teach in a New Digital Landscape" (2010), Roland emphasizes the ways that digital media can allow for communication and sharing of information. He points to his own survey work that indicates that many art educators use the internet to research artists and art techniques, but that the interconnected qualities are typically less utilized:

> The potential of the Internet as an innovative learning tool for students to post their work to the Web for feedback, design their own websites, explore virtual worlds, engage in socially responsive projects, or exchange work and collaborate with students in other schools or countries, has yet to be realized in many art classrooms today (p. 18).

The reasons for this disparity are complicated, and Roland suggests that art educators can expand the uses of digital media through the integration of digital media including open source and free software and rethinking the ways that digital and traditional media overlap. Two years later, Castro (2012) reported on a study of social media use by high school students who engaged with one another through a private password-protected network. Castro uses complexity theory to inform the study of these interactions and suggests that art educators might use social media in much the same way as Roland.

When these papers were written, there were numerous disparities that excluded certain groups of young people, which is known as the *digital divide*. For example, in the US in 2011, 92% of children aged 0–8 from homes making more than 75,000 dollars a year had high speed internet access at home, compared with 42% of children of the same age group from homes that made less than 30,000 (Rideout, 2017). In the decade after Roland wrote about Web 2.0 and Castro reported on social media use, networked digital media has continued to proliferate. During this time, the presence of mobile media in all homes doubled, and the use of these devices tripled with the same age group (Rideout, 2017). Here, I must address how the term *use* is being used. It is not clear, from this study, what is meant by mobile media use. With regards to art educational practices, it would be illuminating to know how these young people are using these media. Does use mean watching YouTube videos? Playing mobile games? Taking photographs? Drawing using an app such as Loop, Penultimate, or Procreate? Each of these activities surely can be seen as having a connection to artistic expression. Even the example of watching YouTube videos is not a purely passive act; as I discussed in Chapter Four, YouTube and social media in general build in modes of interaction such as the ability to "like" or "dislike" content, as well as the option to comment on posted videos, engaging with creators and consumers alike.

De la Rosa-Carrillo (2015) makes the argument that internet memes should be thought of as a viable approach for conducting arts based educational research. As he states:

> Researching Internet Memes by generating Internet Memes forces the researcher to consider them not only as the passive result of a social phenomenon that is played out in the digital realm, but as a craft and a language: a visual medium demanding to be engaged on its own terms (2015, p. 190)

In design education, it has been argued that the study of memes can help designers who focus on digital user experiences, or UX (Adamska, 2019). These arguments for social media as artistic medium should be compared to Roland (2010) and Castro (2012), who argue for the use of social media in the communication about works of art. Both positions are important to consider. However, these applications of social media tend to treat social media as either a platform for communication or an artistic medium. As I have shown through the works of digital visual art previously discussed, social media works to unsettle previous binary relationships, and presents challenges for artists and educators that are altogether new. In terms of the relationship between internet memes and pedagogy, Bristow suggests the following: "What memes can and do teach us is that the very dialectic between form and content is structural, and in its effects is material" (2019). In this manner, the making of memes in terms of form is probably simpler than the creation of content. This represents a shift in the ways that making is often viewed in art education especially in PK-12 settings. In these settings, content is generally less important than form, where learning skills and applying various techniques is emphasized. For memes to be taken more seriously by art and design educators, it is important to identify and analyze the specific attributes of memes as they relate to artistic production and distribution. The attributes of digital virality that I previously identified will now be used to explore potential applications in a Digital Visual Art Education. These are collectivity, mutation, and circulation.

Collectivity is commonly thought of as a process by which a group shares in the process of authorship or production in general. As I suggested earlier in this chapter, this can be connected to the notion of digital visuality, where the means of production are clearly marked and easily accessed. This access makes the work more easily produced and distributed in a collective manner.

However, the collectivity that the internet meme represents is something a bit more complicated, as Wark and Wark (2019) argue:

> The Internet meme is produced by a collective. This collective is constitutive of its capacity to be produced as a plurality and to mutate as it's produced in common. But who are the "we" who constitutes this collective? It appears as a plurality of user positions, all formally the same, all of more or less troubling or compromised authenticity (p. 308).

This is a form of collectivity that echoes the description of the dividual proposed by Deleuze (1992). As discussed in Chapter Two, the dividual is the product of the societies of control that allow freedom of movement or block access through passcodes. In the process the previous binary split between individual and mass enforced through Modernism is unsettled.

Here, the internet meme can be seen as a manifestation of the challenges to Modernist forms of subjectivity brought about by social media. What does media studies, or art and design education have to add to this conversation? As I discussed in Chapter Two, the subject is an important element within many art educational practices and approaches. De la Rosa-Carrillo (2015) connects the shifting subjectivities found in internet memes to Actor-Network-Theory (ANT):

> The idea of making objects accountable in ontological terms resonates loudly with ANT's own stated purpose of keeping the social flat so that all actants are revealed as part of actor-networks that are always in flux and making each other act (p. 69).

While this is a theoretically-sound statement, Latour states that ANT is not a social theory, as social theory has historically privileged the human over the non-human (Latour, 1996). If we sideline this concern, we nonetheless can see that the ways that internet memes are generated can allow art and design educators to consider ways of making that are not traditional, as they entail the collective processes of a variety of actants.

The second aspect of internet memes that should be drawn into a relationship with art educational practices is mutation. Mutation relates to the indeterminate variability of meme generation, where components are recombined in numerous ways, and with a variety of effects. Mutation is related to variations that take place in a given artistic style or predetermined media. For instance, the famous chart made by Alfred Barr for the book jacket of the text Cubism and Abstract art (1936) frames artistic creation as a process of influence. Barr's chart maps the influences that form the movements of Cubism,

Fauvism, and the like. However, this pre-digital data visualization is a creative interpretation, and not an assessment of these relationships based upon quantified data. Placing the information in a graph-form makes the connection to scientific research, and with it the status of quantifiable information.

There is an understandable urge to map the various ways that internet memes proliferate. Just as in the chart made by Barr, the diagram has the power to clarify relationships and define larger forms of influence. In this manner, Yoon (2014) analyzes the process by which racist memes mutate and proliferate. In this research, she suggests that art educators can critically deconstruct such memes using a Visual Culture-based media analysis. This process has the potential to contribute to an understanding of how memes mutate, and, if expanded into related conversations about digital images in general, the ways that such images are uniquely created and distributed within networks of digital technologies.

Yoon (2014) offers a poststructural analysis of memes as related to racism. However, in this study, the visual qualities are not fully addressed. She does state that art educators can help students to make memes that counter racist ideologies: "Since Internet memes have the power to engage students in the art-making process, art educators should be involved in creating them" (p. 117). However, she provides few details as to how this is to be done. More specifically, the work of De la Rosa-Carrillo (2015) points to the challenges of making memes in the space of art and design education, particularly when considerations of style and technique are involved. The automated process of meme generation enters the maker into conversations about originality and uniqueness in potentially intriguing ways. Art, design, and media educators who are interested in making art in and through social media must come to terms with these issues, if they are to truly address the unique and compelling qualities of internet memes.

Circulation relates to the interconnected reflexivity of digital visuality, as the process of replicating memes creates both individual memes while it impacts larger groups of memes that are related. As Wark and Wark (2019) note: "Circulation is constitutive of the Internet meme as thing: the Internet meme can't be collectively produced and can't mutate unless it circulates" (p. 302). Internet memes tend to circulate within the environment that they are produced, although in rare cases, they cross over into other media and platforms. This can be seen in the example of Pepe the Frog, which became infamous in 2016. In the run up to the US election in that year, Pepe was licensed by its creator, Matt Furie, to be used in video games and on clothing

(Furie, 2016). It was also used by racists and white supremacists to spread bigotry and sow division, to the point that Furie, mounted a campaign to rebrand Pepe (Furie, 2016). The hashtag #SavePepe was created, but the damage was done. Furie killed off Pepe in 2017, drawing him in a comic book distributed during Free Comic Book Day where he was laid to rest in an open casket (Hunt, 2017).

Art, design, and media educators who see such complex issues in the teaching of digital visual culture can learn much from internet memes, especially those that speak to political and social issues. March (2013) presents an analysis of memes related to the Jerry Sandusky child abuse scandal at The Pennsylvania State University, studying the ways that user-generated memes are shared and commented upon through the social media platform Facebook. This study treats memes as a product of the amateur artist, looking to internet memes less as a form of artistic expression and more as a form of visual propaganda. Inevitably, internet memes are both, and can speak to the ways that the internet is used to collectively produce, mutate, and circulate digital visual images.

The work of Donnett (2011) and Russell (2020) speaks clearly to these attributes of internet memes. Acknowledging the unique qualities of internet memes can engage art, design, and media educators in important conversations about race, power, and political engagement. An analysis of social media in general can also lead to important discussions of creation and distribution in networked digital media, discussions that can speak to the benefits as well as the dangers of such spaces. The research of Roland (2010), Castro (2012), and De la Rosa-Carrillo (2015) each offer art and design educators unique options for engagement with and through social media. Yoon (2016) and March (2013) speak to the analysis of social media forms, and specifically internet memes, that can inform art and design educational practices at many levels.

Data Visualization and Digital Visual Art Education

There are a number of artists and groups that have been discussed in previous chapters that utilize data visualization in their artistic practices. Within the context of educational research, Andrea Polli's Social Media Workgroup

(SMW), founded in 2009 at the University of New Mexico looks to establish an academic locus for the study of art and social media:

> Frustrated with conventional ways of teaching art, technology, and media that I saw as a factory creating consumers of commercial products, I decided to create a research group that would not only work at a high level of art, design, and programming, but would approach work in electronic and social media with a critical eye. I believed that the definition of the social media, co-opted by Myspace and Facebook, needed to be reexamined. In other words, the lowercase 'social media' term might be complemented by an upper case 'Social Media' through which each term could be expanded upon as technological tools, ideas and users continually evolve. (2014, p. 504)

The SMW stands as an example of art educational practice that looks to the social and cultural impact of social media that extends beyond its embeddedness within specific devices or technological platforms. Many of their projects use data visualization to communicate complex or otherwise unnoticed environmental concerns such as clean air and carbon emissions. Their research goals are as follows:

1. Development and presentation of informed strategies for art and environmental science collaboration
2. Analysis of concrete situations and existing practices
3. Design of encounters and events
4. Evaluation of social media for their contributions to changes in cultural practices
5. Hands-on exploration of the function of various social media works as drivers or catalysts for social change. (p. 505)

The SMW represents an interdisciplinary, collective approach to artistic research that aligns with many current approaches in higher education. However, these approaches could just as easily be applied to other sites of art education, including PK-12 public schools, community centers, and museums. Goals one and three would be quite applicable in these sites. Although number three is broad in scope, it describes much of what happens in the spaces of art and design education in general. The fifth goal is more specific, and as such could drive art educational approaches to learning that are informed by the dynamic qualities of social media, while at the same time using such media as an element of the work.

As mentioned earlier, the SMW use data visualization as a strategy to make visible processes that often go unnoticed. As the primary investigator in the SMW, Andrea Polli also uses similar strategies in her personal work. One such project is called *Particle Falls* (2015–present) which measures particulate matter in the air and displays the results in real time as a light projection in public spaces. *Particle Falls* (2015–present) has been presented in Philadelphia, Pittsburgh, and Detroit. In each of these locations, the specific aspects of the air quality change the way that the projection appears. As Polli states: "I like to think of these projects as living things that are evolving. I'll show them more than once, and with each iteration it may change" (Yoerger, 2013, n.p.). In the process, a feedback loop is created between the projection and the viewer, who is prompted to consider the impact that they have upon the air quality in their location.

As I have discussed, interconnected reflexivity is an important aspect of understanding digital visual art in a Digital Visual Art Education. *Particle Falls* (2015–present) visualizes this quality through the feedback loops described by Polli. *Particle Falls* (2015–present) also presents the viewer with a way to understand the way that digital visual art is indeterminate, as well as intersectional. This project is different depending on where it is installed, which speaks to indeterminacy. It also outlines issues related to air quality and socioeconomic status. In locations that are densely populated, the air is more polluted. As Cucuzzella (2021) writes:

> The problem depicted in the visualization is part of a much larger problem, that stems from municipal planning practices, and one that cannot be solved through an individual's choice of mobility alone. This is a systemic and structural urban problem, one embedded in the form and services of the city. In this case, the traffic in Los Angeles, where this work was first displayed, is the worst in the world, and inhabitants of the area regularly worry about the level of toxins in the air… the Particle Falls projection is simply conveying what is already widely known, and, in this case, what is already visible through the level of traffic, even if the air toxicity may be invisible. The waterfall is thus didactic and provides a clear message to the public but does not go far enough in helping them understand what can be done to improve the level of toxins in the air. The region's environmental breakdown and overextended car use cannot be improved by citizens alone, as it requires overarching shifts in urban planning and design strategies that are the purview of the experts in the municipality (n.p.).

In *The Dark Database* (2021), by Dennis Delgado, we have seen how data visualization can point to educational applications of digital media that are interconnected, indeterminate, interactive, and intersectional. In this work, the references to traditional Western photographic portraiture are brought into a relationship with contemporary cinema and surveillance technologies.

These are reflexive connections that point to the notion of remediation. *The Dark Database* (2021) is a work that is visually indeterminate, in the sense that the subject is not clearly visible. This form of digital visuality is related to the poor image (Steyerl, 2009). In the poor image, a low-resolution image destabilizes the narrative that the digital image is always the best quality, is always crystal clear. This concept is also related to readings of the digital that are related to class and race. And last, *The Dark Database* (2021) can be read through theories of intersectionality, as the faces that the software is able to recognize are primarily lighter skinned. The erasure of brown and Black people from the synthesized images are a statement on the erasure of brown and Black people from positions of power in the United States, and perhaps from positions of prominence in digital visual art.

Art, design, and media educators have not yet come to terms with these modes of interaction as they relate to data visualization, perhaps due to the commercial nature of data visualization, or the connotations of data visualization as being represented in popular media forms such as the evidence walls in popular entertainment. Another reason for this reluctance to integrate data visualization is that such ways of making run counter to the traditional ways of making and sharing art and works of design in educational settings. Klein (2014) offers one relevant suggestion, as she argues that art educators might address social media use through content curation and data visualizations:

> Visual art educators are uniquely positioned to be the creators of curated content and visualized data due to their attraction to and knowledge of visual images and social media. The ability to recognize and interpret patterns and to use such skills to predict and understand current and past trends, suggest future trends, and influence others using social media will be important for 21st-century visual art educators.

Post-digital Materiality and Digital Visual Art Education

As stated in Chapter Four AI-based works of digital art harness the capabilities of large-scale computing networks and databases to allow the generation of images from text prompts. Programs such as Stable Diffusion, Midjourney and DALL-E have been used to create images by only entering a few key words into a search engine, and the program produces the resulting image or images. In design education, discussions of AI tend to take the form of instructional support. Tang, et al (2022) describe the application of AI in the teaching of animation design strategies. Anderson (2019) outlines the ways that design schools are implementing AI and machine learning, both in how these systems are designed and how they might be implemented in educational settings. AI in these cases is an extension of computer-assisted pedagogies that have existed for decades.

As a developing area of artmaking at the time of this writing, few art educators have presented research on the implications for AI-based works of digital visual art and art educational practices. There are, however, a few notable exceptions to this. Chiu, et al (2022) describe the potential for AI-based instruction in art educational practice. Slotte Dufva (2023) argues that a technological feminist stance can allow for the critical evaluation of AI art. He looks to digital visual artists such as Hito Stereyl who subvert the power of computational processes found in AI, proposing a complementary notion of "Artificial Stupidity" (p. 187). And Pente, et al (2023) look at the ethical implications of using AI in educational settings, citing a variety of documents that outline the possibilities as well as limitations of such use in preK-12 school settings from a variety of cultures and locations.

Pente et al (2023) use a posthumanist framework as they analyze these aspects of AI-based art. As I have discussed previously, posthumanism acts as a necessary corrective to descriptions of human-technology interaction that center the human and disregard or downplay the nonhuman. New Materialism provides a framework through which the complexities of AI-based art might be better understood. Art educators Garnet and Sinner (2019) argue a similar point related to the telling of stories in educational contexts. In a New Materialist framework, the fact that the human is collaborating with powerful databases and coding languages would not be seen as a form of dehumanization. In this manner, New Materialism can be seen as correlative to Actor-Network Theory of Latour (1996). The collaboration between machine systems, code, and humans actants creates a network of interactions that are to be acknowledged without the judgment that accompanies humanist notions of individuality or creativity.

We can come to similar conclusions when we consider aspects of human-machine-code interactions as they relate to Non-fungible Tokens, or NFT's. NFT's operating as extensions of established art markets, emphasizing rarity and monetizing uniqueness. NFT's might have a role to play a role in maker education, allowing learners to better understand somewhat esoteric aspects of computing such as blockchain technology (Hwang, 2022). However, the implications for art and design education are still to be determined. Regardless of how NFT's evolve and intertwine with art, design, and media education, digital technologies are continuing to perplex many and captivate many more. Educators in these fields should pay close attention to developments in AI and blockchain technology, as they directly impact digital visuality and digital visual artmaking.

Makerspaces and Digital Visual Art Education

Art, design, and media education all share a focus in looking at various forms of making. In addition to explorations of cognition and critical viewership, contemporary art, design, and media educational practices demonstrate the many forms that making can take in the art classroom, museum space, or community center (Sweeny, 2017). Halvorson and Sheridan (2014) propose three components that can frame future research and exploration of maker culture in education. These three components are: "making as a set of activities, makerspaces as communities of practice, and makers as identities of participation." (n.p.).

The first component is the act of making. As mentioned earlier, making in art education has been centralized, emphasized, reconceptualized, and criticized at various moments throughout the history of the field. Currently, making in art education is being rethought by art educators who are interested in big ideas (Walker, 2004) design-based approaches (Vande Zande, 2007), as well as digital ways of making (Knochel & Patton, 2016). There are numerous ways of making that are championed in the maker movement. These relate, in equal measure, to themes found in art, media, and design education. Making in many makerspaces draws from traditional techniques such as woodworking and screen printing, which are often combined with circuitry and computer programming. The accessibility of newer technologies such as 3D printing and Arduino programming have brought high-tech ways of making to a broad audience. These are the devices that Giertz taught herself to use, and that can be integrated into educational settings with no need for vast readjustments to space or skillsets. Makerspaces draw equally from high-tech and low-tech traditions, with the hopes that the variety of ways of making can meet the needs of the users. As Peppler and Bender (2013) write: "This high-low-tech integration is characteristic of the maker movement" (p. 26).

Art, design, and media educators may find that makerspace-based approaches are easily incorporated into educational practices, as both tend towards ways of making that are similar. Just as art educators integrating maker-based concepts and approaches would have to reconsider the process by which art is made, and even suspend the judgment of what is created as being art, they would also have to rethink the spaces of art, design, and media education. The field of art education has often been wary of an overdependence upon digital technology, as Gregory (1996) suggests. This is at odds with the maker movement, which tends to lean towards the fetishization of digital technologies and technological gadgets (Smith & Light, 2015). If art, design, and media educators are to incorporate ways of making derived from the maker movement, they will have to come to terms with this discrepancy. In addition, the ways that educators share the products of this making would also have to be rethought. Works that incorporate a variety of mechanisms, and that rely upon a performative element, such as switching on a servo motor or interacting with a motion-sensitive device, would require an appropriate venue for display. The static artistic displays common in community, museum, and preK-12 settings would inevitably have to change. This change could be quite productive, as art, design, and media educators might reinvigorate practices that have become predictable.

The issues that Peppler and Bender (2013) raise emphasize the role that individuals play in establishing and maintaining makerspaces. They also emphasize the difference in the basic structural aspects of makerspaces and educational settings. However, this account tends to overlook the companies and organizations that have marketed the maker movement, rebranding the term *making*, where makerspace products and approaches are designed and sold with the intent of framing the process of making in prescribed ways. While this may be the inevitable result when DIY movements become popular, it does not diminish the possibilities for makerspaces in educational settings, if one acknowledges that change is an inevitable by-product of this incorporation.

In this last component, the title of maker should be compared with the equivalent from the fields being discussed here: artist, designer, or media artist. This is the component that demonstrates the most difference. While both are interchangeable, they refer to cultural experiences that are quite unique. A maker is one who makes, while an artist is one who makes art, a designer is one who designs products, and a media artist makes media productions. The differences are one of degree. While all make, an artist, designer, and media artist all create a specific product that exists within a defined social and historical framework. This leads to my last recommendation regarding the discussion of makerspaces as they relate to Digital Visual Art Education. Art, design, and media educators should maintain the tradition of scrutinizing what it means to be an artist, designer, or media artist, even as materials change and new techniques are created. In order to sustain this tradition, such educators can rely upon the myriad examples of artists that come from community settings, diverse cultures and time periods, and contemporary, emerging practices, including but not limited to digital media.

Digital Visual Identity and Digital Visual Art Education

The emphasis on identity has been central to many different forms of art, design and media education practices through time and across space. From early 20th century child-centered approaches inspired by developmental psychology (Stankiewicz, 2001; Wieder, 1998), through Discipline-based Art Education (DBAE) in the mid-20th century, art educators have often focused on artmaking as a form of individualism. As National Art Education Association (NAEA) President Reid Hastie stated, in 1959:

> The task of the art educator is to nurture the artist in each of us by promoting the habit of creativeness. Through valid art experience, the individual can gain satisfaction from invention and exploration and become sensitive to relationships. As these goals are realized the self-dependent desire of the individual will be able to persist in spite of the inter-dependent requirements of our society and will keep pace with dynamic changes in our physical world. The art educator is aptly suited to meet this challenge. As an artist, he [sic] is personally and intimately acquainted with the struggle to produce a comprehensive visual statement of his times. As a teacher, he [sic] is in touch with society and understands the spirit of a people… their hopes, uncertainties, searchings, and successes. It is the art educator's responsibility to bring forth a new sense of the individual in a turbulent society (p. 5).

Design education is closely tied to the field of art education. The history of design education parallels the history of art education in the United States, as both were tied to early forms of industrialization and social mobility. However, design education has been marginalized, as Levy (1990) suggests:

> Design, as a distinct discipline, has rarely sought to develop knowledge constructs within which the activities of thinking, planning, creating, and producing artifacts

> could be shown to be tributary to epistemic principles. Instead (and this is perhaps overly simplistic), design knowledge has been doggedly maintained as merely a form of tacit knowledge, based primarily on knowing how things work. Although this view may seduce the impressionable, it is a view of design inordinately limited in intellectual content and stiflingly reductive in terms of organizational structure (pp. 42–43).

There remains a divide between art and design as they are arranged in academic situations. The simplistic overview is that both are spaces where things are created and ideas are developed, but art education deals with forms of expression, while design education focuses on the application of techniques and principles (Findeli, 2001). Identity, therefore, is not seen as a relevant aspect of the design process, although researchers such as Levy (1990) aim for this to change.

There is a similar conflicted relationship between the notion of identity and practices in the field of media education. Media education and its related set of approaches known as media literacy do not exist as a formal set of practices in the same way as art education. As Jenkins, et al (2009) state:

> Media education is taking place for some youths across a variety of contexts, but it is not a central part of the educational experience of all students. Our goal for this report is to encourage greater reflection and public discussion on how we might incorporate these core principles systematically across curricula and across the divide between in-school and out-of-school activities. Such a systemic approach is needed if we are to close the participation gap, confront the transparency problem, and help young people work through the ethical dilemmas they face in their everyday lives. Such a systemic approach is needed if children are to acquire the core social skills and cultural competencies needed in a modern era.

Here, identity is framed through the concepts of ethics and cultural competencies. These are concepts that are also emphasized in art education, but media education and media literacy tend to focus on the individual as receptor of information, and not the maker. Jenkins' (2009) notion of *participatory culture* unsettles this binary as it deals with concepts such as remixing and modifying, which impact the user in important ways.

The relationship between the individual and the society as framed through art, design, and media education should be addressed as it relates to digital visual identity. The "inter-dependent requirements of our society" as noted by Hastie (1959) are described as forces that threaten the individual. This is a centralized diagram where the individual is the center, and social influence spreads out around the core. This diagram is common in many of the artforms of the mid-20th century, including but not limited to the writings of authors such as Ayn Rand and the critical interpretation of the paintings of Jackson Pollock.

This statement speaks to a general concept of identity that may be dated, and it is certainly not one shared by all contemporary art educators. While this is the case, there are aspects within this conceptualization of the individual that have been maintained in the fifty years since this was originally stated. In the 2015–2020 NAEA Strategic Vision, the relationship between the individual and the society is framed as such: "Increase and bond community through a shared commitment to the NAEA mission and vision—building collaborative relationships with individuals and organizations" (n.p.). Here, collaboration is emphasized, where in the Hastie statement, the individual is placed in an adversarial relationship with society.

It is important for art, design, and media educators to explore how contemporary identity is formed and maintained, especially in a globalized context. The aspects of identity that I have identified—individualism, language, capital, and gender—have the potential to open up important conversations in the spaces of art, design, and media education. First, notions of individuality in these fields should address the influence of digital technologies. The landmark work of Turkle (1985, 1995) speaks to identity as it is formed by networked digital technologies. Specific to the discussion of YouTube as platform, Duncum (2014) argues for the relevance of YouTube as a site for expression and critical engagement in art educational practices. More generally, art educators Garoian and Gaudelius (2004) speak to her work and how it relates to the ways that digital technologies and the human body mediate one another:

> The body constructs technology and technology constructs the body and identity. Notwithstanding one's genetic predispositions, "who one is" and "what one says and does" is conditioned by an interplay of various cultures, namely through institutions such as government, family, schooling, religion, commercial media, and advertising. Each of these institutions deploys regimes of technology to mediate one's life. Such issues as mediation and the relationship between technology and identity are often controversial and difficult (p. 51).

This is what Deleuze (1992) calls the *dividual*. Where Garoian and Gaudelius see opportunities for resistance, Deleuze offers little hope that these forces can be warded off. In Raunig (2016) however, we see a description of the *dividual* that makes use of this fragmentation, channels it and redirects the force in the General Intellect. Art, design, and media educators who are studying digital technologies must content with these sociocultural forces, regardless of their choice to use digital technologies as an artistic medium.

Second, the relationship between identity and race is a common theme throughout the history of art education, at least since the 1980's, when multicultural approaches were first introduced (Delacruz, 1995). Art educators such as Song (2009) have written about the importance of artmaking in addressing identity as related to culture and ethnicity. However, the relationship between ethnicity and digital technologies in art educational practices have only recently come to the fore with the acknowledgement of globalization, as Delacruz (2009) contends:

> New technologies facilitate such caring and doing in ways unimaginable a generation ago, promoting new forms of creative expression and inquiry about diverse art and other forms of creative cultural expression and social action, networking across spans of time and distance, and moving classroom learning into the global public sphere (p. 16).

With this networking comes the opportunity for new forms of cultural expression that can be both positive and negative. Art, design, and media educational researchers should continue to scrutinize the colonialist influence of digital technologies and social media platforms as they continue to evolve and proliferate. This is particularly important within the spaces of networked digital technologies, as they historically were thought to have the potential to be free from biases based in forms of traditional identity such as ethnicity.

Third, the relationship between contemporary capital, class distinctions, and education should be explored by art educators who are invested in the critical examination and implementation of digital visual media. jagodzinski (2005) has placed the use of digital technologies in art education within this capitalist framework, offering the following warning:

> Art education should not place its stress primarily on the tools of technology for mainly narratological representational purposes so as to aestheticize the self even more clearly, for this is the hyper-lure that the new technologies of designer capitalism seductively offer (140).

It is not clear exactly what jagodzinski means by "aestheticize the self" in this passage, which is drawn from an essay on Virtual Reality (VR). However, in many of his writings, he is quite critical of the influences of what he terms *designer capitalism*, which functions as an offshoot of visual culture. Here, VR is scrutinized for the high-tech surface effects that it can produce. And while the aspirational potential of VR continues to blossom evergreen, accessible technologies such as YouTube continue to spread rhizomatically.

As I have discussed through the work of Raimundi/Chuleta and Musson/Youngman, YouTube videos can be relatively low-tech, challenging new media slickness through post-digital practices. These require only a simple smartphone and an internet connection to post videos. Regardless of the trappings, jagodzinski's concern applies to YouTube as well, in terms of how the platform allows one to aestheticize the self. In this manner, the Marxist analysis of digital labor on YouTube Andrejevic (2009) is also relevant. The ability for social media platforms such as YouTube to mine the data of its users is consistent, whether they are watching a home-made makeup tutorial or a million-dollar blockbuster film. The historical forces that have suppressed the economic gains of women in particular are fully operationalized in the monetization of content on YouTube.

This leads to my fourth, and last, aspect of digital visual identity, and how it relates to art educational research practices. Gender is certainly an important component of contemporary identity. As I have discussed, gender is framed in very specific, provocative ways in the YouTube videos of Raimundi/Chuleta and Musson/Youngman. In my previous example, Liao (2010) has encouraged her students to analyze forms of gender representation of avatars in digital spaces, teasing out provocative aspects of such representation and how they might be addressed through pedagogical means.

Digital technologies have long been discussed in extreme terms, as either social evil or utopian panacea. The true nature of digital technologies is, of course, open to debate, and extremely subjective. In the case of digital visual art on YouTube, these forms continually change along with larger cultural shifts. Representation is just that: Re-presentation. And when one re-presents themselves, they may be able to exercise some level of control over the process, as well as the product. Self-representation in a digital visual culture must acknowledge the complicated nature of identity. Art educators conducting research, artists making art, and media theorists teaching about these topics should be aware of the ways that individuality, race, commerce, and gender intertwine and connect, sometimes in ways that are harmonious, and sometimes in ways that are conflicting. Regardless of the impact on the viewer, these forms of self-representation should be acknowledged as facets of curious, complex and critical moments related to a Digital Visual Art Education.

Videogames and Digital Visual Art Education

Contemporary videogames have been discussed and debated in numerous academic fields. The widespread engagement with videogames has led to the creation of new fields such as Videogame Studies:

> Broadly stated, video game studies is the academic analysis of various aspects of computer, console, arcade, and Internet games. It is frequently an interdisciplinary field of study, with scholars from film and media studies, popular cultural studies, American studies, psychology, sociology, education, and literature departments writing about and critiquing games and gaming. Video game studies fall primarily into two main academic camps: social sciences-based studies and humanities-based studies. Social science-based game studies look at the ways that games and gaming affect people, and how people make sense of and interact with games. Humanities-based game studies examine the meaning and context of the games themselves, either in terms of the narratives created and possibly created by video games, or by the unique possibilities for analysis presented by the interactive nature of video games (Konzack, 2007).

While this last point is debatable, it is worthwhile to think about the ways that different disciplines approach the study of videogames. Instead of trying to present an overview of these studies, which are vast and have been described in more detail in previous publications (e.g. Wolf & Perron, 2003), I would like to instead focus on the ways that these fields address the visual qualities of videogames, and how these qualities relate to the aspects of digital visuality that I have been developing in this book.

The first quality of digital visuality is interconnected reflexivity. As previously discussed, interconnected reflexivity is the aspect of digital visual art related to the multiform ways that contemporary digital media intertwine and interact. In this process of intertwining, the work of digital visual art allows the viewer to reflect upon aspects of their engagement, including their identity. In the case of videogames, the player is provided with the opportunity to engage in this reflection. As previously discussed, Interactive Fiction games such as *Depression Quest* (2013) rely upon a reflexive form of engagement that allows the player to empathize with the protagonist in the game.

The intense relationship between the player and the characters in many contemporary videogames foregrounds this reflexive process, to the point where many players closely identify with characters in the game. This is a process that can be viewed as empowering, as Gee (2008) contends. However, it can also be interpreted as a negative form of identity dissolution, very much in line with the history of moral panics related to media use by young people at various points in the past (Markey & Ferguson, 2017).

There are important parallels between the current moral panic related to videogames and those related to previous media forms. As Lupton and McDonald (2010) state:

> Perhaps the most recognizable similarity between novels and videogames in their respective moments of escalating popularity lies in the panicked responses they have provoked. Today's games have been charged in the popular press with blurring the distinction between fantasy and reality to the point of disrupting the productivity, obligations, and mental health of their consumers. The fear games provoke in the popular imagination, like the similar fear provoked by the first wave of popular novels in the eighteenth century, is closely linked to this critical assessment of immersion.

This is an example of the necessity for Digital Visual Art Education to draw from related fields such as media studies. Without this perspective, art, design, and media educators would not get a sense of the multilayered historical influence that plays an important role in how digital visual art is made, used, and understood.

In terms of a Digital Visual Art Education, it is useful to look at the issue of reflexivity in all of its complexity as it is related to art, design, and media education. In the field of art education, there have been numerous scholars who have written on the topic of videogames. Within these, there are a few notable writings that look specifically at the issue of reflexivity and identity. jagodzinski (2007) discusses the general issue of the utility of videogames in education:

> As "pure" entertainment, videogames appear to be the antithesis of the serious business of education. Although creative play has always been part of educational discourse, most often easily justified and contained within the confines of elementary grades where such rhetoric can still sell, its binary opposite—work—begins to dominate as the pressure to find a job in the social symbolic order becomes more and more pronounced and pressing in high school and later in postsecondary institutions.

jagodzinski also poses the question about the interactivity that videogames enable and how this form of reflexive interaction raises serious issues about the interrelationship between creativity, violence, and the ethical force of art. His description of the subjective options afforded the player of the game is somewhat negative, especially when compared with Gee (2008). While this may be the case, he certainly does not fall into the trap of superficially looking at surface attributes of videogames such as graphics or game narratives. He also does not assume that videogames are yet another moral panic. His analysis, informed by the work of Lacan, provides educators, and art educators specifically, with much needed perspectives on the reflexive relationship between games and identity.

In the area of design education, direct application of methods and techniques are commonly emphasized. This is, in part, due to the influence of the applied arts upon design education (Findeli, 2001). While this might be the case, there are numerous design educators who are looking to sociocultural issues as related to the design of products and experiences. Squire (2006), for example, argues for looking at videogames as designed experiences precisely because the cultural influence that they carry relies upon reflexive interactive experiences:

> If a hallmark of games is their interactivity, their ability to grant players agency within the narrative fiction of the gameworld and its rules, then theoretical models need to account for players' actions in creating the experience. Indeed, because play is instantiated only through players' actions, tensions arise over who exactly is the "author" of the game experience (p. 21).

In media education, videogames have typically been viewed as media forms that are passively experienced. However, contemporary networked digital media provides numerous options for the creation of agency in gameplaying as well as gamebuilding. As Kafai and Peppler (2011) state: "Today youth not only consume media when browsing the Internet and sharing information on social networking sites, but they also produce content when contributing to blogs, designing animations, graphics, and video productions" (p. 89). These are reflexive forms of interaction where the process of creating the product changes the producer.

The second aspect of digital visuality that should be discussed as it relates to videogames is indeterminate variability. Indeterminate variability deals with the structure and function of the digital visual artwork, and how this structure changes as the work is presented, viewed, and used. In the case of *Depression Quest* (2013), the experience of playing the games changes depending upon where the game is played, who is playing the game, and by the choices made within the game. Both diegetic and extradiegetic aspects of gameplay further increase the variability of the experience, as Galloway (2006) argues.

In art education, there has been some discussion of the variability that videogames enable, and how this relates to making and understanding art.

Patton (2013) argues for a game-based pedagogy in art education that focuses on making games as well as playing games, for the following reason: "Games, specifically video games, display potential to provide meaningful learning experiences for youth, yet most educational research has related directly to the learning that stems from game-playing" (p. 36). In his approach, complexity theory is used to describe the variability of the experiences that are supported through videogame. Patton also argues that making videogames can demystify the process by which games are made, which can empower art students to use similar strategies in life.

In design education, the variability of videogame experiences is often addressed through the related fields of User Experience (UX) and User Interaction (UI). However, the modernist roots of design education have hampered the ability for design educators to expand the possibilities of the field into those that are more egalitarian and related to the common experiences of the user (Michl, 2007).

In media studies, material variability in videogames and how it relates to similar dynamic forms of interaction in novels has been explored by researchers such as Lupton and McDonald (2010). They situate the history of materiality in the concept of remediation:

> One way to explain why producers of popular entertainment might risk drawing attention to the materiality of their own work in this way is to describe it in terms, not of transcendence, but of "remediation." Media theorists Jay Bolter and Richard Grusin have coined this term as a way to describe explicitly the phenomenon by which new technology encompasses and references existing forms of representation in order to promote the transparency of a new medium while exposing the mediatedness of another, normally older, style of representation.

Remediation is a concept that can be useful for art, design, and media educators who are interested in a number of aspects of Digital Visual Art Education. The concept is particularly relevant for the discussion of digital media in general, as it challenges the perpetual claims that new technologies have been developed without previous precedent or influence. In the discussion of videogames, it is necessary to understand the ways that videogames developed from previous computer games, as well as computer simulations and visualizations, and games in general.

The third aspects of digital visuality related to contemporary videogames is intersectional power. In this concept, the influence of social and cultural forces is acknowledged and analyzed, with the hopes that they might be better understood. In art education, there have been theorists who have looked to the social themes within videogames, and the implications for the players. Parks (2008) argues for a social reconstructionist approach to using serious games such as *Darfur is Dying* (2006) in art educational settings. As she writes:

> Video games and gaming have remained largely unexamined by art education scholars. Additional research is necessary to understand the role of new media and youth, particularly in regard to video games like Darfur is Dying, and art education that is reconstructionist (p. 246).

While this has changed somewhat since the time it was written, the nature of technological process in videogames means that there are always new genres of videogames to examine. For example, the genre of mobile gaming was not a popular form in 2008. In 2020, mobile gaming made up 57% of the global videogame market, representing a larger share than console and PC games combined (Businessweek, 2020). It is in mobile gaming that art educators may find numerous opportunities for fruitful connections to the histories of performance art, happenings, as well as digital visual art in general (Sweeny & Patton, 2009). In *Domestic Tension* (2005), we can see the influence of performance art and first-person shooters being brought together in compelling ways.

In design education, there has been recent interest in what is called culture-oriented product design. As Deserti and Rizzo (2014) state:

> Some scholars introduced the idea of "culture-oriented product design," or the idea that culture can be seen as a catalyst for designing innovative products if and when designers are able to incorporate a specific culture into the product design, thereby giving space to the interpretation of local characteristics, in contrast to the globalization of solutions. This line of thinking can be associated with the vast literature on the reasons and modes of making design interact with the context of destination, primarily but not only represented by the end-user, thus leading to solutions that properly fit a specific context. If we assume that designers should focus not just on the needs but also on the culture of the end-user, we get to the idea of "culture-oriented product design" (p. 43).

Culture-oriented product design acknowledges the needs and desires of the specific user. In videogame development, this specialized form of design can allow for the intersections of identity forms to be incorporated into the game itself. This can allow videogames to speak to power imbalances as they are structured through social structures and products. In both *World of Awe* (2005–present) and *Domestic Tension* (2005), the gameplay is directly impacted by the ability for the player to connect through high-speed internet. This is a form of power imbalance that is related to the notion of the digital divide. *Depression Quest* (2013) does not rely upon elaborate graphics, but the ability to play still requires a reliable internet connection and adequate software.

Videogames have historically been considered as forms of entertainment, and as such have been either excluded or marginalized in the fields of educational research in general, as jagodzinski (2007) and Patton (2013) claim. In media studies, videogames have been generally incorporated into discussions of previous media, as mentioned earlier through the concept of remediation. As Bogost (2011) theorizes:

> One way to make games more ordinary and familiar is to help them realize their place in meaningful art and culture. Indeed, that's the primary strategy one finds in the commercial game industry. Whether successful or not, the industry strives for Hollywood blockbuster–style spectacles. The fledgling indie game scene often privileges new gameplay mechanics or subjects for games, but just as frequently it showcases the hopeful yet derivative swing of so many minor leaguers trying to break into the majors. Despite major differences, both efforts trace the earnest hope that videogames are an expressive medium as important and viable as film or literature, but different in form. It's a fine goal. But as videogames become more familiar, they also become less edgy and exciting (p. 150).

This process of familiarization and the dulling of excitement that follows is a challenge for art, design, and media educators who are hoping to integrate game design in their practices. The ability to maintain a high level of excitement while also drawing out fruitful conversations about class, race, and gender is a tall order to be sure. The Quest to Learn middle and high school in Manhattan is a unique project that is attempting to fuse the cultural relevance and engagement of contemporary videogames with the learning outcomes associated with game-based learning. Funded in part by the MacArthur Foundation, Quest to Learn is led by New York City educator Elisa Aragon and Parsons Professor of Design and Technology Katie Salen-Teknibas, and features an interdisciplinary curriculum based upon games and learning. This curriculum looks to video games both specifically and broadly, exploring how game-based experiences relate to systems thinking and complexity theory.

Patton (2013) also has identified educational value in the relationship between videogames and complexity theory. The interconnected, indeterminate, interactive, and intersectional qualities of contemporary videogames certainly make them relevant resources for art, design, and media educators.

However, there are aspects of videogames as digital visual art that certainly change as they are integrated into educational settings. This is the challenge for all educators who are working in the arena of Digital Visual Art Education. It is my hope that the theories discussed here can provide such theoretical support for educators, designers, artists, and theorists.

If we think about these qualities as related to *Depression Quest* (2013) we can see specific opportunities as well as challenges for practitioners in art, design and media studies. First, we can see that videogames such as *Depression Quest* (2013) do not fit neatly into the category of videogames that have been viewed as a media panic. Supposedly violent videogames are seen as having a negative influence on the player, or, at best are just a waste of time. As jagodzinski (2007) theorizes, the latter type of games represents a type of nonproductive time that short-circuits the neoliberal education system which seeks to quantify productivity in learning. *Depression Quest* (2013) would not probably be seen as violent by media critics; it might be seen as a waste of time, on the other hand. Either way, the interconnected reflexivity of videogame play is central to the experience as a work of digital visual art.

It is easy to think of videogames as stereotypical experiences where a lone individual, usually a white male teenager, plays alone. This is a vision of videogame play that is still prevalent, but increasingly less so. Art, design, and media educators should recall that videogames entered the popular cultural imaginary through shared social spaces—arcades—before they became fixtures in homes and handheld devices. This type of performance might have shifted into online forums and the private space of the home. However, educators can respond to the dynamic possibilities of social gaming, allowing for digital visual work to be made and played in social space, and for competition to develop, both between viewers/players and works themselves.

Second, videogames such as *Depression Quest* (2013) create indeterminate experiences for the player. The narratives and the forms of interaction that videogames present are inherently variable, based upon the specific input of the player and the choices that are afforded them by the game designers. In art education, Patton (2013) has argued for the inclusion of game design in art curricula, due primarily to the connections between the procedural aspects of game design and the decision making that everyday life entails. In media education, videogames represent forms of potential empowerment, which aligns with the aims of the designers of *Depression Quest* (2013). However, it is also possible that gameplay here might deviate from the intent of the designers, due to this variability. For example, players might make decisions in the game that are random or are intended to place the protagonist in peril.

Along these lines, digital visual artists should continue to make work that responds to the continuing media forms represented by videogames. Games such as *World of Awe* (2005) draws upon the history of digital media and the ways in which identity and the body is rethought through interface and interaction. Artists can also problematize the verisimilitude of advanced gaming platforms by taking up the glitch as it is depicted in this game. In a similar manner, *Domestic Tension* (2005) uses the shared history of the first-person shooter as it confuses the divide between public and private space. While gameplay has changed through the introduction of physical interfaces such as the Nintendo Wii, there are numerous possibilities for experimentation along the lines of interface and interaction.

Third, videogames are influential forms of cultural power that cannot be easily ignored. The influence of *Depression Quest* (2015), and the disruptions caused by the related series of Gamergate incidents, shows that contemporary videogames speak to audiences beyond those in the gaming community. Gamergate specifically demonstrates the work that needs to be done in gaming communities that continue to harbor sexist and racist beliefs. The intersectional aspects of contemporary videogames are opportunities for educators to addresses issues related to identity formation such as gender, race, and class.

Digital visual artists allow for the rethinking of media at numerous levels and multiform ways. The artists discussed in Chapter Four provide novel reinterpretations of videogames, and in doing so, point to new ways of interacting and engaging with the digital world. In turn, videogames can provide art, media, and design educators with a way of seeing not only digital visual works of art, but the world in general.

Towards a Digital Visual Art Education

My recommendations for art, design, and media educators who are engaging with digital visual works of art in research and practice are as follows. First, such forms of engagement must take into consideration the unique forms of visuality associated with digital visual works of art. Digital visuality is both theoretical and structural. It is theoretical in terms of the content of the work, the intent of the artist, and the interpretation of the viewer. And it is structural as it relates to the form of the work, and the mode of presentation.

Artists, educators, and researchers who are engaged with digital visual works of art should take into consideration these traditions as they study that which is currently emerging. Artists, educators, and theorists who are researching digital works of art should consider the ways that digital visual artists leverage the dysfunctional aspects of vision; the limits of what can be seen, as well as the ways that such limits might point to new forms of visuality as well as visibility. A Digital Visual Art Education must acknowledge the aspects of digital visual art that are visible, as well as those that operate below the surface of the visible.

Next, art, design, and media educators should consider the four aspects of digital visuality that I have proposed: interconnected reflexivity, indeterminate variability, interactive play, and intersectional power. Interconnected reflexivity must be seen as an important element in the study of digital visual works of art, in both the process of making as described by Wilson & Wilson (1977) and in the creation of curricula (May, 2011). The variable and indeterminate nature of digital works of art can offer artists, educators, and researchers numerous avenues for exploration and inquiry. They should look specifically at the ways that digital media open possibilities for new forms of visuality while they foreclose upon others. Data fetishization is also an issue in public education, where students are tracked and monitored with increasing frequency and precision. Art, design, and media educators have the ability to speak to these issues through practices that identify and critique such monitoring, especially when it becomes overbearing. In interconnected reflexivity we can see that the ways that internet memes are generated can allow art and design educators to consider ways of making that are not traditional, as they entail the collective processes of a variety of actants, using a term from Actor-Network-Theory (Latour, 1996).

Indeterminate variability is the next aspect of digital visuality that art, design, and media educators should consider. Educators from these fields have not yet come to terms with these qualities as they relate to data visualization, perhaps due to the commercial nature of data visualization, or the connotations of data visualization as being represented in popular media forms such as the evidence walls in popular media. Another reason for this reluctance to integrate data visualization is that such ways of making run counter to the traditional ways of making and sharing art and works of design in educational settings.

Post-digital practices are also tied to the concept of indeterminate variability. Post-digital works of art stand to change many aspects of art education that incorporate digital technologies and techniques. A Digital Visual Art Education should address these practices, as they create openings for the incorporation of digital processes where the emphasis on relentless progress and mastery is subdued. Art, design, and media educators should pay close attention to developments in AI and blockchain technologies such as NFT's, as they will continue to impact digital visuality and digital visual artmaking. In terms of makerspaces, art, design, and media educators can learn much from the aspects proposed by Halvorsen and Sheridan (2014): making as a set of activities, makerspaces as communities of practice, and makers as identities of participation.

Interactive play is the third aspect of digital visuality that can inform a Digital Visual Art Education. Art, design, and media educators can respond to the dynamic possibilities of video game play and development, allowing for digital visual work to be made and played in social space, and for competition to develop, both between viewers/players and works themselves. The intersectional aspects of contemporary videogames are opportunities for educators to addresses issues related to identity formation such as gender, race, and class in important cultural and social ways.

Intersectional power is the fourth aspect of digital visuality that can help to inform a Digital Visual Art Education. Digital visual identity should be acknowledged by art, design, and media educators, as this concept can allow them to explore how contemporary identity is formed and maintained, especially in a globalized context. The aspects of identity that I have identified—individualism, language, capital, and gender—have the potential to open up important conversations in the spaces of art, design, and media education. Intersectionality highlights the ways that forms of identity interrelate and offer educators the chance to allow students to respond to these intersections in creative and critical ways.

As I conclude this book I will return to the social events that I described in the forward, and that provided much of the inspiration for my emphasis on digital artists of color. COVID-19 is still spreading across the globe, although new variants are proving to be less deadly. Black Lives Matter is continuing to demonstrate for equal rights, even as Black men continue to be killed by law enforcement. The beating death of Tyre Nichols in Memphis, Tennessee in January 2023 has shown that police reform is still an urgent matter in the United States, as is criminal justice reform. It is not clear that art can alleviate suffering caused by institutionalized bias and hate, but digital visual art can provide openings for expression and cultural criticism as shown through the numerous digital visual artists discussed in this book.

Tyre Nichols death was captured by Memphis Police body cameras. This brutal footage should be placed into a visual lineage that includes pre-digital forms of visuality such as lynching photos. This would align with the argument presented by Legacy Russell in *Black Meme* (2020). This video footage exists in the same digital sphere as the videos of Tyre skateboarding when he was younger, which were uploaded to YouTube after his death. Tyre was also a photographer, and his personal website shows scenes from Memphis nightlife and images of sunsets and public murals. These forms of digital visuality are each very different. If art, design, and media educators would acknowledge this difference, then perhaps the limited and inherently dehumanizing media narratives about Black men in the United States might be corrected. It is my hope that social justice can be achieved in the United States by attending to our similarities as well as our differences. By attending to the sociocultural aspects of digital visual art, we might be able to reach a point where interconnections are identified, indeterminacy is valued, interactivity is scrutinized, and intersectionality shows the necessity for power to be equally distributed.

However, as Keith and Mendhi Obadike ask in the digital visual work titled *My Hands Wishful Thinking* (2001): "I still want to know why this happened."

References

Abreu, M. A. (n.d.). Online Imagined Black English. In D. Howard (Ed.), *Arachne #0— – On Gender, Labour and Technology*. Retrieved from https://arachne.cc/issues/01/index.html

Adamska, B. (2019). *Memes as a Tool for Learning UX. Believe It or Not*. Accessed May, 2023, from https://uxdesign.cc/ux-and-memes-260d35b83e68

Andersen, M. (2019). How Design Schools Are Keeping Up With AI and Machine Learning. *Adobe XD Ideas*. Accessed January, 2023, from https://xd.adobe.com/ideas/principles/emerging-technology/ai-education-in-design/

Andrejevic, M. (2009). Exploiting YouTube: Contradictions of User-Generated Labor. In P. Snickars & P. Vonderau (Eds.), *The YouTube Reader* (pp. 406–423). Stockholm: The National Library of Sweden.

Baran, P. (1964). On Distributed Communications Networks. *IEEE Transactions of the Professional Technical Group on Communication Systems*, *CS-12*(1). RAND Corporation.

Berger, J. (1970). *Ways of Seeing*. Penguin.

Blandy, D. (2009). Democracy 2.0. *Studies in Art Education*, 50(2), 107–109. Retrieved October 23, 2020, from http://www.jstor.org/stable/25475893

Bogost, I. (2011). The End of Gamers. In *How to Do Things With Videogames* (pp. 147–154). University of Minnesota Press. http://www.jstor.org/stable/10.5749/j.cttttmwd.24

Bristow, D. (2019). Introproduction. In D. Bristow & A. Bown (Eds.), *Post Memes: Seizing the Memes of Production* (pp. 17–24). Punctum Books. https://doi.org/10.2307/j.ctv11hptdx.3

Bryson, N. (1988). The Gaze in the Expanded Field. In H. Foster (Ed.), *Vision and Visuality* (pp. 91–94). Seattle, WA: Bay View Press/Dia Art Foundation.

Businessweek. (2020). *Global Mobile Gaming Market Report 2020: Worth $98 Billion in 2020, the Mobile Gaming Market is Forecast to Grow to $272 Billion by 2030*. Accessed June 23, from https://www.businesswire.com/news/home/20210625005180/en/Global-Mobile-Gaming-Market-Report-202-Worth-98-Billion-in-2020-the-Mobile-Gaming-Market-is-Forecast-to-Grow-to-272-Billion-by-2030---ResearchAndMarkets.com

Castro, J. (2012). Learning and Teaching Art Through Social Media. *Studies in Art Education*, 53(2), 152–169. Accessed from http://www.jstor.org/stable/24467884

Chiu, M., Hwang, G., Hsia, L., & Shyu, F. (2022). Artificial Intelligence-Supported art Education: A Deep Learning-Based System for Promoting University Students' Artwork Appreciation and Painting Outcomes. *Interactive Learning Environments*. https://doi.org/10.1080/10494820.2022.2100426

Cucuzzella, C. (2021). Making the Invisible Visible: Eco-Art and Design against the Anthropocene. *Sustainability*, *13*(7), 3747. https://doi.org/10.3390/su13073747

De la Rosa-Carrillo, E. L. (2015). *On the Language of Internet Memes*. The University of Arizona, ProQuest Dissertations Publishing, 3703692.

Delacruz, E. (2009). Art Education Aims in the Age of New Media: Moving Toward Global Civil Society. *Art Education*, 62(5), 13–18. Retrieved September 28, 2020, from http://www.jstor.org/stable/20694786

Deleuze, G. (1992). *Postscript on the Societies of Control* (pp. 3–7). October 59. MIT Press.

Deserti, A., & Rizzo, F. (2014). Design and the Cultures of Enterprises. *Design Issues*, 30(1), 36–56. http://www.jstor.org/stable/24267024

Duncum, P. (2014). Youth on YouTube as Smart Swarms. *Art Education*, 67(2), 32–36. Retrieved October 23, 2020, from http://www.jstor.org/stable/24766141

Emme, M. (2001). Visuality in Teaching and Research: Activist Art Education. *Studies in Art Education*, 43(1), 57–74. https://doi.org/10.2307/1320992

Findeli, A. (2001). Rethinking Design Education for the 21st Century: Theoretical, Methodological, and Ethical Discussion. *Design Issues*, *17*(1), 5–17. http://www.jstor.org/stable/1511905

Freedman, K. (2003). *Teaching Visual Culture: Curriculum, Aesthetics, and the Social Life of Art*. Teachers College Press; NAEA Press.

Freire, M. & McCarthy, E. (2014) Four Approaches to New Media Art Education, Art Education, 67:2, 28-31, DOI: 10.1080/00043125.2014.11519262Furie, M. (2016). Pepe the Frog's Creator: I'm Reclaiming Him. He Was Never about Hate. *Time Magazine*. Retrieved from https://time.com/4530128/pepe-the-frog-creator-hate-symbol/

Garnet, D., & Sinner, A. (2019). The Story Object: Embodying (New) Materiality in Teaching and Learning. *Counterpoints*, 528, 51–61. http://www.jstor.org/stable/45178416

Garoian, C. (2010). Drawing Blinds: Art Practice as Prosthetic Visuality. *Studies in Art Education, 51*(2), 176–188. Retrieved October 21, 2020, from http://www.jstor.org/stable/40650461

Garoian, C., & Gaudelius, Y. (2004). Performing Resistance. *Studies in Art Education*, 46(1), 48–60. Retrieved from http://www.jstor.org/stable/3497095

Gee, J. P. (2008). Learning Theory, Video Games, and Popular Culture. In Drotner, K. & Livingstone, S. (Eds.), *The International Handbook of Children, Media and Culture* (pp. 196–210). Sage.

Giertz, S. (2018). Why You Should Make Useless Things. *TED Talk*. Accessed June 22, from https://www.youtube.com/watch?v=c0bsKc4tiuY&t=112s

Gregory, D. (1996). Art Education Reform: Technology as Savior. *The Journal of the National Art Education Association* 49(6), 49–54. https://doi.org/10.2307/3193623

Halverson, E. R., & Sheridan, K. (2014). The Maker Movement in Education. *Harvard Educational Review*, 84(4), 495–504.

Hastie, R. (1959). *The Individual and Society*. Art Education (12.6) National Art Education Association. Stable URL https://www.jstor.org/stable/3184391

Hunt, E. (2017). Pepe the Frog Creator Kills Off Internet Meme Co-Opted by White Supremacists. *The Guardian*. Accessed from https://www.theguardian.com/world/2017/may/08/pepe-the-frog-creator-kills-off-internet-meme-co-opted-by-white-supremacists

Hwang, Y. (2023). When Makers Meet the Metaverse: Effects of Creating NFT Metaverse Exhibition in Maker Education. *Computers & Education, 194*. https://doi.org/10.1016/j.compedu.2022.104693.

jagodzinski, J. (2005). Virtual Reality's Differential Perception: On the Significance of Deleuze (and Lacan) For the Future of Visual Art Education in a Machinic Age. *Visual Arts Research, 31*(1), 129–144. Retrieved September 28, 2020, from http://www.jstor.org/stable/20715374

jagodzinski, J. (2007, Spring). Videogame Cybersubjects: Questioning the Myths of Violence and Identification (Implications for Educational Technologies). *Alberta Journal of Educational Research*, 53(1), 45–62.

Jenkins, H., Purushotma, R., Weigel, M., Clinton, K., & Robison, A. (2009). *Confronting the Challenges of Participatory Culture Media Education for the 21st Century*. MIT Press.

Klein, S. (2014). Making Sense of Data in the Changing Landscape of Visual Art Education. Visual Arts Research, 40(2), 25–33. https://doi.org/10.5406/visuartsrese.40.2.0025

Knochel, A. (2013). Assembling Visuality: Social Media, Everyday Imaging, and Critical Thinking in Digital Visual Culture. *Visual Arts Research*, 39(2), 13–27. University of Illinois Press.

Knochel, A., & Patton, R. (2015). If Art Education Then Critical Digital Making: Computational Thinking and Creative Code. *Studies in Art Education*, 57(1), 21–38.

Konzack, L. (2007). Rhetorics of Computer and Video Game Research. In J. P. Williams, & J. H. Smith (Eds.), *The Players' Realm: Studies on the Culture of Video Games and Gaming*. London: McFarland and Company, Inc.

Levy, R. (1990). Design Education: Time to Reflect. *Design Issues*, 7(1), 42–52. https://doi.org/10.2307/1511470

Liao, C. (2010). Avatar as Pedagogy: Critical Strategies for Visual Culture in the Virtual Environment. In Sweeny, R. (Ed.), *Inter/Actions/ Inter/Sections: Art Education in a Digital Visual Culture*. NAEA.

Lupton, C., & McDonald, P. (2010). Reflexivity as Entertainment: Early Novels and Recent Video Games. *Mosaic: An Interdisciplinary Critical Journal*, *43*(4), 157–173. http://www.jstor.org/stable/44030298

Lupton, D., & Williamson, B. (2017). The Datafied Child: The Dataveillance of Children and Implications for Their Rights. *New Media & Society*. Accessed from http://journals.sagepub.com/doi/full/10.1177/1461444816686328

Manovich, L. (2001). *The Language of New Media*. MIT Press.

March, L. (2013). *Memes to an End: An Analysis of Online Activist art from the Penn State Blue Out Movement to End Child Abuse*. Masters Thesis. Penn State University.

Markey, P., & Ferguson, C. (2017). Teaching Us to Fear: The Violent Video Game Moral Panic and the Politics of Game Research. *American Journal of Play*, *10*(1), 99–115.

May, H. (2011). Shifting the Curriculum: Decentralization in the Art Education Experience. *Art Education*, 64(3), 33–40. Retrieved October 23, 2020, from http://www.jstor.org/stable/23034053

Michl, J. (2007). *The Case against the Modernist Regime in Design Education*. Accessed June 22, from https://www.janmichl.com/eng.apartheid.html.

Miller, P. (2004). *Rhythm Science*. MIT Press.

Mirzoeff, N. (Ed.) (1998). *The Visual Culture Reader*. Routledge.

Nakamura, L. (2007). *Digitizing Race*. University of Minnesota Press.

Parham, J. (2020). TikTok and the Evolution of Digital Blackface. *Wired Magazine*. Retrieved from https://www.wired.com/story/tiktok-evolution-digital-blackface/

Parks, N. S. (2008). Video Games as Reconstructionist Sites of Learning in Art Education. *Studies in Art Education*, 49(3), 235–250. http://www.jstor.org/stable/24467881

Patton, R. M. (2013). Games as an Artistic Medium: Investigating Complexity Thinking in Game-Based Art Pedagogy. *Studies in Art Education*, 55(1), 35–50. http://www.jstor.org/stable/24465508

Pente, P., Adams, C., & Yuen, C. (2023). Artificial Intelligence, Ethics, and Art Education. In A. Knochel & O. Sahara (Eds.), *Global Media Arts Education: Mapping Global Perspectives of Media Arts in Education* (pp. 197–211). Palgrave Macmillan.

Polli, A. (2014). A Walk in the Woods: Investigating Ethical Design, Ubiquitous Computing and Social Media. *Leonardo*, 47(5), 504–505. Retrieved December 1, 2020, from http://www.jstor.org/stable/43832968

Raunig, G. (2016). *Dividuum: Machinic Capitalism and Molecular Revolution*. Semiotext(e).

Rideout, V. (2017). *The Common Sense Census: Media Use by Kids Age Zero to Eight*. San Francisco, CA: Common Sense Media.

Roland, C. (2010). Preparing Art Teachers to Teach in a New Digital Landscape. *Art Education*, 63(1), 17–24. https://doi.org/10.2307/20694809

Sandell, R. (2009). Using Form+Theme+Context (FTC) for Rebalancing 21st-century Art Education. Studies in Art Education, 50(3), 287–299. http://www.jstor.org/stable/40650338Sharon, T., & Zandberg, D. (2016). From Data Fetishism to Quantifying

Selves: Self-Tracking Practices and the Other Values of Data. *New Media & Society 2017, 19*(11), 1695–1709 https://doi.org/10.1177/1461444816636090
Slotte Dufva, T. (2023). Entanglements in AI Art. In A. Knochel & O. Sahara (Eds.), *Global Media Arts Education: Mapping Global Perspectives of Media Arts in Education* (pp. 181–196). Palgrave Macmillan.
Smith, A., & Light, A. (2015). *How to Cultivate Sustainable Developments in Makerspaces*. Paper Presentation for Center on Innovation and Energy Demand. Retrieved from http://steps-centre.org/wp-content/uploads/MC-report_final.pdf
Song, Y. (2009). Identity and Duality. *Art Education*, *62*(6), 19–24. Retrieved from http://www.jstor.org/stable/20694798
Squire, K. (2006). From Content to Context: Videogames as Designed Experience. *Educational Researcher*, *35*(8), 19–29. http://www.jstor.org/stable/4124789
Stankiewicz, M. A. (2001). *Roots of Art Educational Practice*. Davis.
Steyerl, H. (2009). In Defense of the Poor Image. *E-flux Journal#10*. https://www.e-flux.com/journal/10/61362/in-defense-of-the-poor-image/
Sullivan, G. (2014). The Art of Research. *Studies in Art Education*, 55(4), 270–286. Retrieved October 26, 2020, from http://www.jstor.org/stable/24465527
Sweeny, R. (2006). Visual Culture of Control. *Studies in Art Education*, *47*(4). Reston, VA: NAEA
Sweeny, R. (2009a). The Pedagopticon. Other Eyes in the 21st Century Classroom. *Journal for Social Theory in Art Education*, *28*. Accessed from https://scholarscompass.vcu.edu/jstae/vol28/iss1/7/
Sweeny, R. (2009b). There's No 'I' in YouTube: Social Media, Networked Identity and Art Education. *International Journal of Education through Art*, 5(2) and 3 Article. Intellect.
Sweeny, R. (2015). *Dysfunction and Decentralization in New Media Art and Education*. London, UK: Intellect Press.
Sweeny, R. (2017). Makerspaces and Art Educational Places. *Studies in Art Education*, 58(4). Reston, VA: Taylor & Francis.
Sweeny, R., & Patton, R. (2009). CitySneak: Play, Pedagogy and Surveillance. In de Souza da Silva (Ed.), *Digital Cityscapes: Reconfiguring Social and Urban Networks via Locative Media*. New York: Peter Lang.
Tang, T., Li, P., & Tang, Q. (2022). New Strategies and Practices of Design Education under the Background of Artificial Intelligence Technology: Online Animation Design Studio. *Frontiers in Psychology*, *13*. Accessed January, 2023, from https://doi.org/10.3389/fpsyg.2022.767295
Tervo J. (2012). The Problem of Representation. *Studies in Art Education*, *54*(1), 81–83. Retrieved October 21, 2020, from http://www.jstor.org/stable/24468132
Turkle, S. (1985). *The Second Self: Computers and the Human Spirit*. MIT Press.
Turkle, S. (1995). *Life on the Screen: Identity in the Age of the Internet*. New York: Simon and Schuster.
Vande Zande, R. (2007). Design, Form, and Function in Art Education. *The Journal of the National Art Education Association*.

Walker, S. (2004). Artmaking in an Age of Visual Culture: Vision and Visuality. *Visual Arts Research*, 30(2), 23–37. Retrieved October 22, 2020, from http://www.jstor.org/stable/20715350

Wark, S., & Wark, M. (2019). Circulation and Its Discontents. In A. Bown & D. Bristow (Eds.), *Post Memes: Seizing the Memes of Production* (pp. 293–318). Punctum Books.

Wieder, C. (1998). Child Art and the Emergence of Learning Styles. *Visual Arts Research*, 24(1), 21–27. Retrieved September 24, 2020, from http://www.jstor.org/stable/20715932

Wilson, B., & Wilson, M. (1977). An Iconoclastic View of the Imagery Sources in the Drawings of Young People. *Art Education*, 30(1), 5–12. https://doi.org/10.2307/3192209

Wolf, M., & Perron, B. (2003). *The Video Game Theory Reader*. Routledge.

Yoerger, W. D. (2013). The Artistic Climate: Andrea Polli Transforms Scientific Data Into Art. *American Artscape Magazine*. National Endowment for the Arts. Accessed from https://www.arts.gov/stories/magazine/2013/3/kind-beauty/artistic-climate

Yoon, I. (2016). Why Is It Not Just a Joke? Analysis of Internet Memes Associated with Racism and Hidden Ideology of Colorblindness. *Journal of Cultural Research in Art Education*, 33, 92–123.

INDEX

E

F

G

H

I

J

K

L

M

N

O

P

R

S

T

V

W

www.ingramcontent.com/pod-product-compliance
Ingram Content Group UK Ltd.
Pitfield, Milton Keynes, MK11 3LW, UK
UKHW020842290926
15470UKWH00004B/1491

9 781433 195648